The Power
the Phone

Tested Techniques to Cut Costs,
Save Time and Boost Sales

■

PAT COCHRANE

the Institute
of Management

PITMAN PUBLISHING

The Institute of Management (IM) is at the forefront of management development and best management practice. The Institute embraces all levels of management from students to chief executives. It provides a unique portfolio of services for all managers, enabling them to develop skills and achieve management excellence. If you would like to hear more about the benefits of membership, please write to Department P, Institute of Management, Cottingham Road, Corby NN17 1TT. This series is commissioned by the Institute of Management Foundation.

Pitman Publishing
128 Long Acre, London WC2E 9AN

A Division of Longman Group UK Limited

First published in 1993
Reprinted 1993

© Pat Cochrane 1993

A CIP catalogue record for this book can be obtained
from the British Library

ISBN 0 273 60211 X (Paperback)

Photoset in Linotron Century Schoolbook by
Northern Phototypesetting Co., Ltd., Bolton
Printed by Bell and Bain Ltd, Glasgow

Contents

■

A telephone audit of your business

Introduction

'People are saying "We want to do it this way!" A lot of our customers want a quick, efficient way of communicating and the telephone provides it. If that's what our customers want, then we have to provide it.'

It is worth noting that the volume of calls made via an 0800 freephone facility increased by 1,000 per cent between 1985 and 1988, with an estimated further 440 per cent increase between 1989 and 1992. The volume of freephone calls rose from 6.9 million in 1985 to 371 million in 1992. BT's own research claimed that six out of ten adults would prefer to respond to an offer by telephone rather than use a freepost coupon. The telephone (which has achieved an overall 91 per cent penetration of the population, rising to 97 per cent of AB socio-economic classes) has replaced the pen as the most popular means of personal communication. When was the last time you wrote a personal letter? When did you last make a personal telephone call? In 1984, only 77 per cent of the population had a telephone.

The increase in the use of mobile telephones underlines the fact that the business community is responding to the need to be instantly accessible to both customers and colleagues. A trend towards replacing written communication with a direct call to businesses is now well established.

HOW IMPROVING THE USE OF THE TELEPHONE CAN HELP YOU

■ You can benefit from taking the time to analyse your company's or department's use of the phone. The skills discussed in the book can be applied to any organisation, in any market.

- You will be advised on how to make the best use of the telephone in all business situations, not just in sales and marketing.

- You can identify business opportunities where telephone and marketing skills can be introduced without risk to your existing customer base.

- You can increase your contribution to the efficiency of your business by speeding up the response mechanisms to queries from your customers.

Opportunities for business

There is no single area of business that is not affected by the use of the telephone. Total Quality Management, Customer Service, Sales, Marketing, appointment making, order taking, dealing with credit enquiries, invoice queries and PR activities all involve the use of a telephone at some stage. Understanding how telephone communication works in your company will help you to improve results in all of these areas. Apart from face to face meetings, this is the closest you will get to your customer. The telephone is an intimate medium and can be used very effectively to communicate with your customer. Unfortunately, the communication your customer may receive may not be the one you intended. The improvement of the use of the telephone in business has to be driven by managers and all too often it is managers who are least aware of the impact that poor telephone use can have. If you have ever joined other managers in conversation, then I am sure you will have witnessed the following scenario:

Two or three managers are sitting in a room and a telephone rings. It is ignored. The telephone is perceived as being intrusive and, after all, there are other people in the organisation available to take the call, aren't there. However, using the telephone well is not just about picking up a telephone, or answering the call within three rings, or being polite on the telephone. The significance of the telephone as a communication medium has to be recognised and following on from that, training is needed to ensure that calls are treated as business opportunities rather than interruptions. Expensive advertising or marketing campaigns very often fall at the last fence. When a customer rings an organisation and the call is badly handled. This is usually because the company has failed to recognise that you never get a second chance to make a first impression. Whenever the telephone is answered in your company, the way that call is handled says as much about your department or your business as any advertising or promotional material can. The following quotes are good examples of the silly things that people say when they are on the telephone:

'I'm afraid everybody's at a sales meeting today – there's only me in the office. Perhaps if you could call back on Monday somebody may be able to help you then.'

'I'm sorry Mr. . . . . . isn't here at the moment – he's just popped out to get some breakfast.'

'I'm afraid we don't do the kind of service you require. However, one of our competitors does. You might do better to ring them.'

'I'm afraid our computer has broken down again. We won't be able to do that for you today.'

3

Unwittingly they manage to transmit an appalling image of a company's efficiency or professionalism. The words make a strong impression simply because they are not accompanied by a smile or a friendly face. They are stark words spoken into a telephone and have a tremendous impact on the caller.

You are now being asked to consider not only how you handle the telephone call, but how telephone calls are handled in your department. In today's market customers are more inclined to pick up a telephone than they are to write if they have a query or wish to place an order. Already many businesses which traditionally communicated by letter with their customers, are now turning to the telephone as a more cost effective and efficient means of communication. A telephone call allows you to talk to your customers and respond as the conversation continues. In a letter you have to decide on the message you wish to convey to the customer and then send that same message to everybody. There is not the same flexibility of allowing you to adjust and adapt the conversation according to the individual needs of each customer. Thus the sorts of businesses which now rely on the telephone to promote their products and services are many and diverse.

'We've all received the double glazing calls. They just annoy you.'

'They will attempt to talk to you on the basis that they know something about your circumstances when clearly they don't.'

'If people have genuinely done some research and they perceive the need that I might have, I don't mind that, except where there is clearly no thought to it. It's just a random call.'

The quotes above illustrate the sort of things poorly trained people do when they ring potential customers. Perhaps the most damage that has been done in introducing the telephone into the culture of the British business has been done by the call techniques adopted by questionable businesses using poor telephone selling techniques to promote their goods. Unfortunately this has had the effect of preventing managers from appreciating just how valuable the use of a telephone in business can be. In its favour, the telephone is cheap, immediate, can cover any geographical area and is an intimate medium – one which encourages customers to talk openly about their wants and needs. What counts against it is its anonymity and it is this that needs to be addressed to ensure the successful use of the telephone in business.

4

Every time you speak either to your colleagues, your staff or your customers, you create an image. To ensure that this image is a positive one you need to consider just how a telephone call represents a business opportunity, or rather an opportunity to lose business as poorly handled telephone calls have a disproportionate, negative impact on the person to whom you are speaking. An ill chosen word will have much more impact when spoken on the telephone than in a face to face situation. Reading the customer's face will give you clues not to what they are thinking, but this is easily achievable via the telephone. You need to develop techniques to help overcome this problem.

The telephone audit (Fig. 1.1) will give you some ideas about how the telephone may be used in your business. There is no single area of business life that does not, at some time, involve a telephone call. Dealing with employees, suppliers, colleagues, customers, generates an image of you and your company. It also presents you with opportunities to reinforce the Total Quality message that you are trying to communicate. By analysing the telephone activity that you undertake as a manager and that your department undertakes for you, you will be able to identify the opportunities that present themselves to you.

If customers regularly ring your organisation to place repeat orders, you could start to think about what sort of buying patterns are emerging and what sort of opportunities there may be for up-selling and cross-selling. Even if your department is not customer-facing, that is to say it does not deal with external enquiries coming into your organisation or does not make external telephone calls to suppliers, it will still be involved in dealing with the internal communication machine in your business. Have a look at how much paper is generated, are there areas where a telephone strategy could reduce the cost of paperwork? Are memos simply being sent to confirm what has already been said on the telephone? Are they really necessary?

Managers in companies often find that they deal with a whole range of telephone opportunities. Indeed their whole working day may encompass talking to any of the people already mentioned above, or dealing with diverse calls into the organisation. The approach to each telephone call and its content will vary according to the situation. A telephone style needs to be created. If you want to give your customers the right impression, you need to consider how you handle these telephone calls. Using the telephone as a business tool and not simply treating it as something that takes up space on your desk will open up whole new areas that can be exploited in order to develop your department and business.

5

Many managers feel more comfortable communicating via the written rather than the spoken word. This is because the written communication can be closely controlled. You can literally dictate the content of the message you wish to convey. However, this is not possible on the telephone. You need to be responsive. You need to be able to think on your feet and to react quickly to any situation which may arise. This is not to say you should be fearful of using the telephone – it is really more a matter of learning how to control that medium as well as you control the written word. The more practice you have the better you will become. Whilst the contents of a letter can be revised and polished until it is ready for publication, this simply isn't possible in a telephone call. What you say spontaneously cannot be unsaid and because you are only using words to convey your meaning with no visual medium to set them in context, you need to be especially aware of the impression that the words you use can have on the person at the other end of the phone.

The growth of advertising which encourages potential buyers to ring with an order, rather than write, is immense. Within the recruitment pages of a newspaper you will see vacancies advertised for people with good telephone sales skills. However, this represents only a small proportion of the business actually done via the telephone. Building up good relationships with your employees and suppliers, as well as presenting an image via the telephone, are equally key activities. Whilst telephone sales has grown into a £3 billion market, this still represents only a tiny proportion of the amount spent on telecommunication as a whole.

Professional and statutory restraints

UNSOLICITED TELEPHONE CALLS

The legal profession is debarred from making cold calls. This is a professional restraint which may be abandoned when, as many think is likely to happen, the legal profession merges with the Accountancy profession. Although this would involve a change in statutory law, it is a move which would be welcomed by both parties as it would increase the level of service they could offer to customers and the general public.

Being subjected to such restrictions makes it even more important for the legal profession to capitalise as much as possible on incoming calls from potential clients who are 'shopping around'. The Institute of Chartered Accountants (ICA) removed the obstacle to cold calling when they changed the Code of Practice over 18 months ago. This has allowed the profession to embrace proactive telephone activity, allowing them to:

- advise clients of the change in the law which may be of interest to them;
- make appointments;
- issue invitations to seminars etc.

This move has been warmly welcomed by the Accountancy profession and one major practice was able to say with conviction that they have gained tangible business results from proactive telephone activity. Good telephone training, combined with a sensitive approach to prospective clients, has led to an increase in their client base and client activity. They found both existing and prospective clients very responsive to their approach.

ORAL CONTRACTS

This is a basic principle of English Law which is so fundamental that it is not based on any specific case or single source. This section deals with clarifying the legal issues surrounding your liability for what your employees say or do on the telephone. The basic essential of any oral contract is that there must be at least two different contracting parties and there must be a consensus of agreement between them that they intend to create a legal relationship. There must be something of value contributed by each party to support the contract (eg a service provided by one party in return for payment by another). The best way to avoid an oral contract coming into existence is to make it clear at the outset of the discussion that regulations are 'subject to contract' or 'subject to confirmation in writing'. This will indicate that such a discussion is not intended to be contractually binding.

The main drawback to an oral contract is that a dispute may arise as to what terms were agreed. It is advisable to create a contract on an oral basis only in the very simplest of cases – where the number of terms agreed between parties is minimal. In case of strong disagreement between parties a dispute may end up in court, in which case the procedure will be covered by the rules of evidence. The general principle here is that **if a contract is in writing, extraneous evidence is inadmissible** 'Extraneous' means anything that does not actually appear in the original terms of the contract.

7

In the case of an oral contract the case will in fact consist of one party's word against the other's but in this situation supporting evidence, such as evidence of witnesses being present during negotiations, will be admissible. It is likely that tape recorded evidence of telephone calls will only be admissible if the parties can both be identified from the tape recording and it has details such as the authentication of the caller's voice or the date of the call. This sometimes gives rise to problems in considering the admissibility of tape recordings. Questions of legality of recordings are separate criminal considerations.

The Interception of Communications Act 1985 – provides protection for the confidentiality of a telephone call. The act makes it a criminal offence for anyone to intercept a telephone conversation improperly. It is not an offence under this law to intercept a telephone conversation provided that *one party has consented to the intercept.*

Oftel (Office of Telecommunications) regulations were reviewed in December 1992 and much tougher rules covering the use of recording equipment were introduced. Oftel's aim is to bring the UK into line with proposed EC (European Community) regulations which, if ratified, will supersede the 1985 Act. The regulations are proposed by the Comité Consultatif Internationale de Telephonie et de Telegraphie (CCITT), an international committee established to promote standards for the development of telephone networks. Recommendations E180 and E182 require the presence of a warning tone to be used if a call is being recorded or intruded upon. Unless this warning tone is heard by parties at both ends of the conversation, they are entitled to expect the phone call to be private.

The EC Technical Standards for PBXs, key telephone systems, ADCs, telephone recording and answering equipment contain a requirement that a warning tone facility is incorporated into the equipment at the point of manufacture.

Confusingly, telephone recording equipment is freely available in the high street and several varieties of telephone recording equipment are supplied with the warning tone inhibited or not installed. Providers of such equipment rarely warn purchasers of the current policy regarding the recording of conversations and even if you are assured that such equipment is approved for connection to a telephone network, the fact is that while its offer for sale or purchase is not illegal, its use is. Because there is no obligation on the part of the manufacturer, wholesaler or retailer to inform purchasers at the point of sale of the limitation of use of such equipment, it is very easy for a person to find himself unwittingly liable for prosecution should the use of such equipment come to the attention of Oftel.

You can apply to Oftel for specific site exemptions where you wish to use such equipment with the warning tone inhibited. However, exemptions are given only in exceptional circumstances and would not be given where you wished to record or intrude on conversations for purposes of monitoring the performance of your people on the telephone.

Oftel regulations apply only to equipment manufactured after 1984, but a note of caution – even if your equipment has British Telecom's approval of its use, it is still illegal if you do not conform to the conditions of the 1985 Act and Oftel's regulations.

'Black box' communication

Employees who are not in the forefront of customer to company communications undervalue and underestimate the contribution they can make to the success of the company. Customer satisfaction starts with how a company responds to a call. Even faulty goods can be forgiven and customer loyalty retained provided the call is handled well. An after sales enquiry or badly handled credit collection call can damage a business relationship for ever. The telephone encourages 'black box' communication – ie no-one can see me so it doesn't matter what I say, how I say it or what I do. A disembodied, uninterested voice says more about your attitude to customers than anything else. Managers in the public sector need to combat poor customer perception and bureaucratic systems. Improved use of the telephone can have a tremendous impact in both these areas. Imagine the perception generated by the following exchange:

Q How long will it take to receive an answer from you?

A How long is a piece of string?

The above is a verbatim example of a conversation between a member of the public and an employee of a local education authority regarding the processing of an application for a grant. What does the answer convey to you? Seven little words that can say so much . . .

Managers often find themselves on the receiving end of a demand to speak to someone in authority. Good telephone skills can minimise this and save valuable management time. Such demands are nearly always precipitated by an employee's telephone response. Time invested in improving the way in which calls are handled will avoid escalation into serious dissatisfaction.

9

Even internally, employees' perception of the efficiency of another department is usually based on how their enquiries are dealt with. The voice and manner of the person who handles the call says as much about a manager as any written communication. Before you can change your staff's attitude towards the telephone, you need to identify what that attitude is. Many people find the telephone difficult to use. Employees may see the telephone as an intrusion into their normal daily life. Some managers are extremely reluctant to take telephone calls and use their secretaries as a means of screening them, if not protecting them, from this unwarranted intrusion.

Start by discussing with your staff any telephone calls that they have made themselves which they can recollect as being good or bad. Almost always, someone will be able to give an example. Perhaps it was a time they queried a bill or rang a shop to establish whether a certain product was in stock. Ask them to analyse that call.

Once they can identify what makes a good call, they can start to develop their own skills. People who are good at face to face communication often find using the telephone difficult. Executives, when faced with the prospect of making calls, can feel uncomfortable using the telephone. Their instinct may be to write rather than ring. One of the reasons for this reluctance to use the telephone is the feeling that one is being 'put on the spot'. You really do have to think on your feet: you cannot hide behind the written word.

Staff will also ascribe their own feelings to others. If they see the telephone as an intrusion, they will think they are being intrusive when they make a telephone call or will be reluctant to accept a telephone call because they do not wish to get involved in a situation which doesn't allow them the opportunity for analysis and objectivity. Whilst great care is given to the construction of letters and their content or how to convey a message in a face to face situation, managers and employees alike will benefit from focusing their attention on how to be effective telephone communicators.

Telephone audit

To help you to identify possible areas which need to be improved, use the 'telephone audit' (Fig. 1.1) that follows, to complete a survey of all the possible activities that you and your staff engage in. Consider the benefits that might be derived from developing your telephone skills to deal with these situations more effectively.

Companies may be inhibited about using techniques to develop their employees' skills because they associate such training with basic telephone techniques, such as answering a telephone quickly or keeping a message pad by the phone. Any further attempt to develop skills may be seen as verging on 'telephone selling' – an approach to customers that strikes terror into the hearts of many organisations.

> *'TQM and telesales skills should be given to every member of a company who has any customer contact whatsoever. I firmly believe that any person who actually speaks to a customer on behalf of a company represents that company, and is effectively a salesperson for that company. To that end, every single customer-facing employee should be equipped with highly developed questioning techniques and the ability to identify a sales need and feed that back to the relevant source for further investigation. Not only does it optimise every single sales opportunity that is likely to be there, but it also gives an extremely professional gloss to the company. To me, TQM is giving everybody who speaks to customers sales skills.'*

TELEPHONE AUDIT	A	B
Desk research		
Telemarketing		
List cleaning		
Direct mail		
Issuing invitations to customer events		
Questionnaires		
Prospecting		
Appointment making		
Customer care calls		
Account management		
Renewing business contracts		
Selling		
Order taking		
Retrieving lost business		
Handling enquiries		
Dealing with complaints		
Invoice queries		
Credit control		
Internal calls		
External calls – customers / suppliers		
After sales service		

If you or your employees are involved in any of the above activities tick column A.

If they are not specifically trained in using the telephone in these situations tick column B.

Fig.1.1 Telephone audit

Telephone sales people and their managers do exist who are successful in helping companies develop and maintain customers. Unfortunately they have been done a great disservice by the extremely amateurish and questionable tactics engaged in by unprofessional companies. Managers who have been on the receiving end of such an experience rightly shrink from inflicting similar experiences on their own customers.

Nevertheless, the newspaper industry, including reputable names in the quality national newspaper markets, has for the last 30 years enjoyed considerable revenues generated by a proactive tele-sales approach. This industry was heavily influenced by Lord Thomson, who introduced the concept into the UK after achieving considerable success abroad.

The development of telephone sales training has adapted to the changing attitudes of both businessmen and consumers towards telephone contact from organisations. The attitude is now much more responsive to customers' needs and it is recognised that a good 'customer relationship' is paramount. It is a short-sighted approach to go for the 'hit and run' school of selling!

12

These comments are not just appropriate to sales that are made via the phone but in all the other areas of the business where you may find yourself speaking to customers, employees or suppliers. The experience of telesales and their whole attitude to communicating via the telephone has some valuable lessons for all parts of your business. Not all situations require the same approach and the ability to set objectives or recognise the opportunities presented by each call involves giving considerable thought to how the use of the phone in your department or business will affect the image you convey to your callers. Outbound telephone activity is a sensitive area for both employees and companies. The perceived, all pervading 'intrusiveness' of the telephone may inhibit the creative use of the phone to achieve marketing or business objectives. Increasing outbound activity should be approached with caution but not naked fear.

Your customers already do business with you, they like you and will respond to your interest. Test the results of outbound calls by conducting some research on your customers: you will be pleasantly surprised by their positive response. Your relationships with customers will be cemented rather than broken up. It is impractical to rely solely on face to face meetings to sustain contact with them. Customers may not see employees from your business for many months at a time.

The customer care cycle will involve telephone contact all the way. From placing orders to taking deliveries, progress chasing, invoice queries, complaints and requests for information: all these are likely to be initiated by telephone calls. Are you equipped to deal with them? Using the telephone more proactively will help you to:

- Increase and improve the level of customer contact in either sales or service situations.
- Reduce the impact that poor customer relations has on a business.
- Reduce your administrative costs.
- Deal with enquiries from members of the public.
- Reduce the amount of time you spend writing letters.
- Enhance the Total Quality performance of your business.
- Build on existing skills to achieve better results.
- Develop your existing relationship with customers.

A telephone audit will help a manager to identify those areas of communication which need to be analysed and improved.

2

How telephone communication works in business

A look at telephone situations

Introduction

The examples of the following different telephone calls you or your staff are likely to become involved in illustrate very clearly that when a telephone rings or you make a call **it is an opportunity to do business.** The following guidelines are not scripts but are structured to help you complete a successful call. Every call that comes into or goes out of your business should be treated as a chance for your company to present itself in the best possible light to your customers. Use the guidelines to help you maximise every conversation you have with customers or prospective customers.

Marketing

DESK RESEARCH

A company used to use the following tactic as part of its recruitment process when looking for sales executives. Towards the end of the interview candidates were invited to go into an office and complete a questionnaire. The office was furnished with only ordinary office equipment. There were no books that would help them. The questionnaires proved to very complex, requiring detailed information about other countries. Most candidates gave up in frustration. The information needed was clearly beyond what would be considered general knowledge. However, one candidate did not. He recognised that the office did contain something that could help him get the answers he needed: a telephone. He simply rang up his local library and got all the necessary information. The company concerned used this exercise to establish whether the candidate was resourceful or not. However, the story also underlines the powerful benefits of the telephone when used for desk research purposes.

More and more companies are recognising the importance of knowing about their competitors, their customers and their suppliers: what their needs and wants are; what their purchasing cycles are and who makes the purchasing decisions.

If the purpose of your call is explained properly it is amazing how helpful companies and individuals will be when it comes to supplying information. Sometimes a manager may simply be seeking to identify who he could best write to on a certain topic. If the organisation is large and complex you may find yourself re-routed through several different departments. However frustrating this may be, if ultimately it supplies you with the information you need your call will have served its purpose. At the very least, it does mean that whatever communication you follow up your call with, whether it's a mailing shot or a letter, it is more likely to land on the right desk.

Due to the spontaneity of the telephone call, the information you receive is up to date. Whilst published information is useful to anybody in business, it is always, by its very nature, at least slightly out of date. If your company is in a business which changes rapidly and suddenly, telephone research can help you keep up to date with market trends.

Other managers who have been in the same situation or who are in a similar market to yourself respond very favourably to requests for information or advice. People like to talk about their own experience or business. You will find that contacting them by telephone encourages them to be more forthcoming and they may even be flattered by your call. A telephone conversation has the advantage of taking only a few brief minutes of the recipient's time, whereas they are unlikely to respond in writing. Asking for information by letter places the 'burden' on them and they might be tempted to delay writing it as they have more urgent demands on their time. In a telephone call you also enjoy the benefit of 'off the record' conversations.

TELEMARKETING

Confusion can exist in certain businesses about what telephone marketing actually is. It could be described as the process by which a company can identify potential markets for their goods or services. Telemarketing can undertake list cleaning and desk research activities. It can then build on that information to make direct contact with your audience and hopefully from that make an appointment for a representative of your organisation. Telemarketing can apply to areas of your business that are involved in prospecting or customer contact in the following areas:

Outbound calls

- Desk Research.
- List Cleaning.
- Direct Mail follow-up calls.
- Contacting leads supplied by field salespeople.
- Prospecting (material may be sourced from directories, newspapers, own knowledge of the market etc.).
- Maintaining contact with existing customers (care calls or account management calls).

Inbound calls

- Fulfilment (responding to customer request for brochures).
- Helplines.
- Order taking.
- Handling sales enquiries (to appointment stage).
- 0800 calls.

I have purposely excluded selling from the above lists. Selling via the telephone requires a different approach to the initial call whether it is inbound or outbound. Some companies have successfully combined the two activities but because selling a product or service requires a depth of knowledge not normally required for appointment making it seems sensible to view selling as development of telemarketing skills.

If your team's objective is to make an appointment, then the following general guidelines will be useful pointers for your team.

Start at the top and work down. Don't be frightened to ask for the Managing Director, or indeed any director who you think may be responsible for the activity which you wish to discuss.

Start the call with a 'verbal handshake' – in other words, take time to establish a rapport. Explain who you are and why you are calling and then follow up this introduction with an interesting question. You could phrase your question around a topic that may be of common interest. This could be gleaned from a newspaper cutting or perhaps a referral – a customer who has asked you to call him, or it may simply be that you already do extensive business with customers who have similar needs and interests to his own.

Don't get into a detailed conversation about your company's goods or services. When the prospect starts asking questions is the time to arrange a meeting with your company's representative.

Even if you don't succeed in making an appointment you will leave an impression of your company behind – make sure it's a positive one!

If your prospect is not in the market, identify when he will be and make a 'diary appointment' to call when you contact him back. This will build up a bank of qualified prospects who you will be calling when the time is right and therefore they are more likely to respond to your call positively.

LIST CLEANING

By list cleaning I am referring not only to lists which companies buy, but also to any information that you may be keeping on your database or, of course, in manual records. The one thing you can rely on is that this information will almost certainly be out of date. Companies move and change addresses. Managers move on to take on other responsibilities, either inside the organisation you last spoke to him at or indeed in another company. If you are planning to write to people on your list, the time you spend on ensuring your information is correct will never be wasted and it is a very cost-effective way of ensuring that you get full value from your list.

Do remember that companies have different titles for similar roles. For example, Executive, Personnel or Director of Personnel, or Director of Human Resources can all apply to the same role. **Always check the spelling of a name even if you think you know how to spell it.** If you are writing a personal letter it can be extremely irritating to the recipient to realise that you have not taken the time to establish how he spells his name, and it implies a careless attitude. Check that the address is correct. It is very easy to fall into the trap of thinking that a company is

17

where you last thought it was simply because the telephone number has not changed.

Most of the details you need to check will be available from a company's switchboard. Avoid wasting a contact's time by checking minor details prior to speaking to him. Your time available to speak to decision-makers is limited and too valuable to waste.

DIRECT MAIL FOLLOW UP

Whilst direct mail has been an established marketing tool for many years, it is only in more recent times that companies have recognised how powerful the direct mail follow up telephone call can be. Not only does it give you an opportunity to talk to the customer about what they thought about the information, questionnaire, literature or brochure that you sent to him but it also enables you to expand and draw attention to subjects you think may be of interest to him. When used in conjunction with direct mail, the telephone call reinforces the message that you have already sent.

People are lazy. They may be interested in the brochure but simply not get round to following it up with a telephone call to you or by filling in a coupon. Managers file away such marketing literature if they feel that it will be of use to them in the future, and then simply forget they ever kept it in the first place. Telephone calls have been known to double the amount of appointments generated from a campaign and certainly contribute just as much in terms of results as the direct mail activity itself. The telephone call will also alert you to any possible problems. For example, if people are not reading the literature, perhaps you need to look at the copy. Or if they are not the people that you wish to communicate with, then your list needs looking at again.

Always make sure that the people who make the calls have been fully briefed as to the objectives of the campaign and that they are familiar with the contents of the literature that has been sent out.

When opening the call, avoid direct questions such as 'Have you read our recent brochure?' The answer will almost invariably be 'NO'.

Try: **'How do you think our new 24 hour service will match your requirements, Mr Jones?'**

TELEPHONE QUESTIONNAIRES

This is the simplest way to establish whether your company is doing the right things for its customers or suppliers.

First of all, decide what information you wish to gather. Is it purely a fact-finding exercise to establish the size and dimension of your market or is it intended to identify areas of potential customer dissatisfaction, or to discover what your customers like about how your company is conducting its business with them? Make the questions brief and try to structure them in such a way that you do not ask leading questions, otherwise the answers will not be valid. Ask questions that can be answered briefly – time on the telephone is limited. Use questions that can draw a response which can be categorised, eg 'Would you say our products are: not satisfactory, satisfactory, excellent?' Use tick boxes to record the customer's choice. Open questions which allow lengthy answers are not appropriate as it will be hard to record them verbatim and you may end up with an unclear picture of where your customers position you in the market.

19

Always give some guidance about how long you expect the call to take. Establish that the person you are calling is free to speak to you. Most customers are happy to participate and appreciate the efforts you are making to improve your service to them. Finally, thank the participant for his co-operation.

If your questionnaire really does have to be complex or lengthy, it is much better to make a telephone appointment with the person whom you wish to question.

Sales

PROSPECTING (THE COLD CALL)

Prospecting for business is probably the one area of activity that usually fills people with dread. The thought of picking up a telephone call and speaking to an unknown person about your company's products or services can be a terrifying prospect to somebody who has not done it before. Take comfort from the fact that the telephone, when correctly used, is an unintimidating, and intimate, medium. People like to talk on the phone. The person you are calling will take comfort in the fact that he has the ultimate weapon – that is, he can put the phone down if he is unhappy with the way the call is going. This happens so rarely that it really isn't a realistic fear on the part of the caller. To quote one sales director, 'When you are fighting the business war, the salesman may have the sub-machine gun that you need to win!' That is, providing you make your call interesting and relevant to him, he will be generally interested in what you have to say. After all, your business has only succeeded by supplying the right products or services. Isn't it true that other prospective customers will be interested in hearing from you as well as your own customers?

One of the benefits of prospecting by telephone is that you can range all over the country. Field sales people can only cover their own specific territory but somebody canvassing on the telephone can be in Glasgow one moment and Devon the next. Therefore you do not have to limit yourself to a geographical territory.

It is important to sound confident. Somebody who is nervous or hesitant about their products or services can give the wrong impression. Enthusiasm about what you are doing is infectious. Try to remember that even if your call isn't successful and doesn't result in an appointment or an order, nonetheless the people making prospecting calls are still projecting your company image to others.

Checklist

- Avoid anxiety. It only indicates that you are more worried about the impression you make rather than your customer's needs.
- Remember that businessmen like to hear about new opportunities.
- Make the call relevant and interesting.
- Be open and honest about the purpose of your call.
- The secretary isn't your enemy, she is your friend. Thank her when she offers to help: explain the purpose of your call but don't sell to her. Secretaries help to organise and plan their employer's day. Screening telephone calls is often one of their duties. It doesn't mean that she will be reluctant to put a call through, only that she needs a good reason!
- Time on the telephone is very limited: don't waste it. Have a clear objective.
- Develop a two way conversation. This is your opportunity to learn something about your customer.
- Structure your call.
  - Introduce yourself and say why you are calling.
  - Gather information.
  - Check your understanding.

   – Discuss how your company can help.

   – Offer something that is interesting and relevant to him.

   – Justify your price (use expressions like quality, value for money) and explain why it represents a good deal for him.

   – Give him a reason to buy.

- Even if you do not at first succeed, use the information you have gathered to plan your next call.

- LISTEN to your prospects' answers – they will give you clues.

- Prospects who are clearly uninterested are not going to respond to your calls. At the very least they will be long term prospects. Respect their decision. You are wasting your time (which is just as valuable) if you pursue them relentlessly.

- Concentrate your efforts where they are going to yield most results.

- Always establish that your prospect is free to speak to you. If he is only half listening you increase the chance of failure.

- Your prospect will be reassured if you offer an alternative time and is far more likely to give you time if you arrange a telephone appointment that is convenient to him.

21

APPOINTMENT MAKING

The whole question of arranging a meeting for your sales executives needs to be approached with empathy, particularly if your customer or prospective customer has no knowledge of the caller as an individual or of the person they will be sending out. It is very important to reassure him. The less intimidating and the less forceful you are, the more likely he is to agree. Your customer will realise that instead of having control as he does using the telephone, it is much more difficult to get rid of somebody once they are in an office. No matter how forceful he is, without being excessively rude, he then finds himself committed to discussing subjects in which he has no real interest, so before he agrees to a meeting he will need to be convinced that it is going to be a worthwhile experience. If you give an aggressive or 'pushy' impression he is far more likely to say no. He will expect the sales executive to use the same tactics and will be reluctant to invite him in.

It is important to establish, therefore, that there really is interest in you or your product and services and that he genuinely wants to discuss it further. There is a school of thought that goes with the thinking that if a representative has an opportunity to meet somebody with whom he thinks he can do business, then it really is up to that representative to close the deal. Would it not be much more productive to know that your representative is going to meet somebody who genuinely wants to take the conversation further than simply an information gathering exercise?

If an appointment is going to require an hour of the businessman's time, it is much better to establish that during the telephone call. It can be very discouraging for sales people going out on an appointment, especially if they are excited about the prospect of meeting the businessman, to then find that he is only prepared to commit himself to a few moments of his time. To do business successfully takes time. If your businessman is not prepared to allow the time that you require to make the sale then there really is no point in pursuing the appointment. This will only lead to unproductive meetings for your customer and the sales executive. You can create the right impression by taking account of the following things:

Some businessmen agree to appointments because they use it as an opportunity to keep up to date with markets and trends. Whilst this is sometimes helpful in making an appointment, you need to take the time to establish that he has a genuine business need which you hope that your company's products or services can answer.

Do not make the mistake of trying to sell at this stage: your objective is purely to create an interest in your proposition. The point at which your prospect begins to ask questions, is the time to introduce the possibility of setting up an appointment with somebody who is well versed in your company's products, ie your sales executive. Check details, such as where your prospect's office is. That is essential to avoid problems. If it is a very large organisation the chances are the site will cover many acres and there may be several different buildings, any one of which could be the one where your prospect actually is. Wherever possible, ask him to fax a map. This may sound basic but many representatives have told the tale of when they have gone out to the wrong address or the wrong site and then started off on totally the wrong foot by being late for an appointment.

Thank your prospect for allowing your company the opportunity to come and talk to him and say that you will be following up your representative's visit with a call to check progress. (Incidentally, these calls can prove to be very productive in other areas. It is a good way of checking that your salesman has arrived on time and has kept his appointment.)

IDENTIFYING A CONTACT'S NAME

From time to time you may come across the problem of someone telling you they are 'not allowed to hand out that sort of information'. Companies who operate this policy risk losing the opportunity to make contact with potential customers and suppliers who may be able to help their business. Its secretive attitude seems rather old fashioned today. However, if you find it difficult to establish a name, there is a technique to help you.

Reassure the person at the other end of the phone that you do not wish to talk to the contact, only to write to him. Say that because you are a professional organisation and naturally wish to address your correspondence to the right person, you want to ensure that his name is spelt correctly. As an alternative you can try a different branch or division of the company and you may be more successful at getting the correct name. Company policy is sometimes the invention of the switchboard.

Once you have the name you require, you can then make another approach and increase your chance of success in being put through by asking for the contact by name. Using this technique is not a guarantee but will increase your success rate.

23

Try to avoid the pitfalls that can occur where the name may be 'unisex', eg Chris or Sam. It is worth checking on gender. Nothing annoys a businesswoman more than being asked by a caller to put them through to Mr Chris . . . on the assumption that she is a secretary. Many a business conversation has got off to a bad start because of this error.

'They will say "I thought it would be a man". They would then ask to speak to a director on occasions as they want to talk to a man. That annoys me very much.'

'Credibility from professional people is not there. Joe Bloggs in the street will accept you eventually but I find that professional people or the junior rank managers do want to speak to somebody higher than me.'

'I sometimes wonder if men have more authoritative voices, just because of the way their voice works. The same with female newscasters – a lot of people say they don't sound as authoritative as men. Maybe that comes across on the phone and it is a perception which continues. On the other hand it could be sheer prejudice.'

Most female managers have suffered the indignity of being mistaken for their own secretaries and no matter how much they protest to the contrary, the fact is that when it happens it does colour their attitude to the proposition in a negative way. A little bit of homework prior to the call will repay handsomely.

Checklist

- Introduce yourself and say why you are calling.
- Use the 'verbal handshake'.
- Tell him which company you represent.
- Ask a question to establish your customer's level of interest.
- Gather information, use open ended questions to help establish a two-way conversation.
- Use his name frequently to establish a rapport.
- Encourage the customer to speak and avoid cutting across replies.
- Always acknowledge an answer before moving on to the next question.
- If you identify an opportunity don't start selling – you will talk your way out of the appointment.
- When the customer starts to ask questions about your product or service, offer to arrange a meeting.
- Explain that your colleague will be better equipped to answer his questions fully.
- Reassure the customer that the meeting will be productive and that your colleague has a professional attitude.
- Tell him about your other customers.
- Offer alternative times.
- Avoid jargon.
- When discussing the length of the meeting, don't use phrases like 'just popping in', 'it will only take ten minutes' or 'he's in your area'. It demeans the meeting for both of you.
- Give a realistic time that you think the meeting will last.
- The meeting will only be worthwhile if your colleague has sufficient time. Any less, you are wasting his time.
- When you make the appointment, check address and location details. Ask him to fax a map if possible.
- Thank him for giving your company the opportunity to talk to him.
- End on a note of confidence that the meeting will be mutually beneficial.

ACCOUNT MANAGEMENT

Account management is becoming more popular. Companies are now recognising that, whilst gathering new business is an essential activity, it is also time consuming and expensive. If too much time is focused on gaining new business, insufficient attention may be given to keeping the business that you already have. Account management will help you do this. It can cost at least five times as much to win a new customer as it does to retain an existing one. Your staff will relate to your customers and that increases customer loyalty. It is not just a handholding exercise, it is a very effective way to increase your profits. Account management plugs the holes at the bottom of the bucket that drain away your profits. It also enables you to form opinions about where your business is coming from. Are there any particular trends? Are there any particular sections of industry or commerce which lend themselves to your product or service? It gives your customers an opportunity to tell you what they want and need. Customers are very favourably disposed to businesses which are keen to retain their business and which show interest in them. By account managing, not only do you keep the accounts you already have, but you cement business relationships.

Sometimes companies are reluctant to undertake this activity as they see it as opening a Pandora's box. Perhaps the customers will have complaints. Surely it is better if they voice their complaints to you and give you an opportunity to find solutions, rather than allowing the account to degenerate to the point where your customer goes elsewhere. Even if you do get involved in handling complaints, this should be treated as a positive thing. After all, the customer has given you the chance to put it right. Where companies have a large customer base, perhaps covering a huge geographical area, the telephone lends itself to this activity very well. Customers don't leave when a problem occurs, they leave when nothing is done about it.

If you have a customer base of, say, 3,000 customers, a team of only two operators can ensure that every single one of them will be rung at least four times a year. This will allow you to plan and take account of situations where perhaps your existing contacts have left the business or a newcomer has different ideas about who should be his supplier. Businesses change every day. They certainly change every quarter. This is the minimum amount of time that you can risk letting lapse before you speak to a customer. I have assumed a 42-week working year to arrive at these figures. If you use as a basic rule of thumb 70 calls and 30 contacts a day, you can quickly identify how many operators you are likely to need to cover your customer base. You may then like to consider segmenting the customer base even more. For example, large customers will need to be rung more often.

Because account management calls are likely to draw very specific enquiries from your customers, it is important that the people you choose to make these calls have the necessary skills. They should be well versed in your own company, with a knowledge of how it operates and who the key managers in the business are. If they are presented with a problem, they need to be able to go some way towards resolving it. At the very least, they should know whom to refer the problem to in order to get a solution. Remember that the people who make these calls are responsible for looking after every single one of your customers. Therefore you need to choose people who not only have an interest in your business but are also able to convey the professional and enthusiastic impression that you wish to communicate to your customers.

Checklist

- Have the customer's records available.
- Use the call to reinforce the relationship with your customer.
- Identify opportunities for up selling and cross selling.
- Check that the customer is getting full value from your company – is he using the right service, contract or product for his needs?
- Check data and ask if there are any other areas of the business which would be interested in talking to you.
- Ask for referrals outside his business.
- If your customer is not spending as much as expected, investigate – competition could be stealing business from you.
- If he is exceeding your expectation is he paying the right price? If he isn't, tell him before your competitors do!
- Ask him to make a note of your name and telephone number. Make yourself easy to contact.
- Prevent small problems growing into major areas of dissatisfaction.
- Ask if your contact's role remains the same. People move on in organisations or take on more responsibilities.
- Talk to everyone in your customer's business who influences, as well as makes, decisions.
- Finish by saying when you will call again and thank him for continuing to do business with you.

RENEWING BUSINESS

Often, renewing business is seen as a separate business activity. If a company is about to come to the end of its contract either with yourself or with a competitor, that puts them in the market for a new supplier. Don't leave it until the contract has run out. Unfortunately this is something that many companies do. Ideally, you should contact him at about the length of time prior to the contract ending that it would take for the buying process to be completed.

However, the competition is out there trying to steal your customers and, whilst you may have an active field sales force, why not reinforce what they are doing with a telephone call. Take this as an opportunity to establish trends. Is your customer happy with your products and services? Are the supplies being delivered on time? Is he likely to be expanding? Will he need more in the future? Try to establish what his buying patterns are and then make sure that you make the call to him before he feels it necessary to make the call to you.

27

SELLING VIA THE TELEPHONE

Many sales directors will have firm opinions about what cannot be sold over the telephone. Telephone sales managers are obviously biased. They believe everything can be sold over the telephone. The truth is somewhere between the two.

If you want people to sell your product or service via the telephone you must ensure that the support systems are in place. Nothing is worse than when a customer says 'Yes' and then nothing happens. If you don't have adequate and efficient support systems you have a problem. That is not to say that these need to be expensive but if other departments are involved in making that process happen, you need to appoint somebody to start that chain going. It should not be the telephone sales operator. They are too busy getting more business for you on the telephone. That is what you want them to do. The paperwork and progress chasing required to effect an order needs to be in place. If letters of confirmation need to be sent out, try to send them out the same day. The same goes for any documentation that may be necessary.

Selling over the telephone isn't all that different from selling face to face, in the sense of the structure of the call. The telephone sales person needs to follow similar patterns. The biggest constraint on them is time. In a face to face situation it isn't uncommon for a meeting to take an hour.

Thirty minutes can be considered the norm. The longest telephone sales call is not likely to take more than ten minutes and on average calls take between three and four minutes. The constraints on time are considerable, so what you have to consider here is how best to use that time.

When training new people a script is useful in that it gives them something to hold onto while they are building up confidence and gaining experience. An experienced telephone sales executive will not need this crutch. Remember that you have recruited them for their communication skills and certainly the receiver of the call has never read your script. If he asks your operator a question that doesn't appear on the script it is desirable that the telephone sales operator isn't thrown off balance. Potential business is sometimes divided in terms of what value it is to the company. For example major accounts will be handled only by field sales executives. Small accounts will be handled only by telephone sales operators. Whilst this has in the past proved to be a useful rule of thumb, it can be true that the bigger the business and the busier a decision maker is, the more inclined he will be to do business over the telephone for the simple reason of expediency. Therefore when deciding what should be sold via the telephone, do take into account that the value of the product or service should not be the main deciding factor. The purchasing manager of a small account may always need to see somebody. The purchasing manager of a large account may not. The important thing is to find out how it works in the company and then match your sales activity to suit.

If the product or service is a complex one, it may be necessary to support your telephone sales executive's activities with brochures or literature. These are expensive to produce and it's worthwhile establishing the level of interest that the prospective customer has before sending these out. They should only ever be seen as supporting weapons in the telephone sales executive's armoury, not as replacing their skills.

Telephone sales executives need to develop communication skills which will enable them to describe the product or service in such a way that the receiver of the call understands what is being sold. They don't have the advantage of being able to use visual aids during a conversation and therefore their skill must be backed up with good product knowledge.

The value of telephone selling has now been recognised by many companies. Today, car hire, distribution, financial services, building societies, mail order catalogues, travel operators are just a few of the businesses who promote and sell their products and services using the telephone. As customers become accustomed to doing business by tele-phone companies are finding it necessary to revise their marketing strategy to adjust to the changing climate.

ORDER TAKING

The moment when a customer places an order is crucial. Customers placing orders via the telephone are sometimes subjected to unnecessary waits and are then told that a product is not available. This has a very negative effect on his attitude towards your business. Your operator should be trained to offer alternatives if something is unavailable. If an acceptable alternative is offered, it might be taken up by the customer and an opportunity to do business is not missed.

If you can turn one order into two, that can only be good for business. Most companies spend a lot of time and money chasing prospective customers, so if they are coming to your door, welcome them in. Don't tell them what you haven't got, tell them about what you have.

29

RETRIEVING LOST BUSINESS

Insurance companies have an expression for policy holders who have fallen through their net. They call them 'orphans'. This doesn't mean that the policy has lapsed but that somehow or other sales people have failed to keep in regular contact with them. This is also a problem for sales managers who are trying to ensure that their sales executives manage their territories and take account of existing as well as new business opportunities. The quiet customers fade away. Orphans exist in many businesses. A sales executive will tell you why he thinks an account was lost. He will describe all the things that went wrong: how other departments let him down; how goods weren't delivered on time or perhaps they were faulty; sales people are good at that. It is true to say that a sales executive working a geographical territory and trying to organise his time to ensure that he has the best business opportunities, thinks that retrieving lost business comes way down the list of his priorities.

A new rapport can be established but it takes time and the people who have the time are the people who use the telephone. They don't have to make lengthy trips to establish contact. Even when business is lost, companies are willing to give a second chance if they truly believe you have learned from the experience. Perhaps since the business was lost you have introduced new management or changes, launched new products or restructured your prices. Any one of a number of things could have happened in your business which, after all, is a dynamic one. Your ex-customer will be unaware of these changes. If you really have worked to solve the problems, then by telephoning him you can open the door again and re-establish contact. You will still have to prove that you deserve his business but at least by telephoning you demonstrate the fact that you want to continue doing business with him.

'Lost business' frequently means 'lost contact'. Keep in touch, keep trying, give the customer a reason to do business with you and he will. Even the most damaged customer relationships can be rescued if you exercise enough care. Although it is tempting to think of dissatisfied customers as a 'lost cause', they did think once that you were the right company to do business with. If you maintain a relationship with them you might rekindle the flame. You start several steps ahead of cold calling because a need has already been identified.

Checklist

- Concentrate on re-establishing a dialogue with your customer.
- Use the call to gain a better understanding of why you lost the business.
- Once you have identified the reason, think about the changes your company has made since you last spoke to him and how they may benefit him.
- You could discuss some of the following: reduced prices, restructured company, new personnel, new management, new products or services.
- Customers are willing to give second chances if you can convince them that you have learnt from your mistakes.
- Keep talking to your ex-customers and you could win them back.

Handling enquiries

The important thing to remember about enquiries is never to take them for granted. An off-hand answer which subsequently proved to be to the wife of a company's major customer had disastrous results. Her husband was the chairman of a company which placed a multi-million pound order with a distribution company to deliver their products. She felt that if her husband's customers were getting the same dusty response to an enquiry about the whereabouts of a package, then perhaps this wasn't a company that he ought to be doing business with. The situation was eventually rescued, but it did tie up senior managers' time for some considerable time.

If the person who handles the call doesn't have the necessary information a satisfactory response is impossible. If you have staff in your department who are likely to receive telephone enquiries from customers or members of the public, you need to consider how best they can handle the situation. Your staff cannot be expected to know all the answers to questions they are likely to receive, but they at least must have the means by which they can seek the answers they need. Staff should avoid passing the call from department to department. Their inclination may be to get rid of a call, not to take ownership of it. Expressions such as 'You need to ring this number' should be avoided. Some companies have recognised this problem. A switchboard is busy with incoming calls and the operator simply cannot afford to get involved in a time consuming enquiry when she knows there are other callers trying to get through. Therefore the temptation to make a hasty decision and guess at the department where the caller should be put through to leads to this long chain. So what these companies have done is to establish a bank of people who can handle these enquiries and give the callers more time and attention.

31

In small companies this isn't always a practical solution as such teams are expensive to run. Therefore, at the very least, what should be available to everyone who takes incoming calls is a list of departments, a brief summary of what they do and the name and telephone number of a person in each department to whom enquiries should be directed in the first instance.

The best way to establish how these calls are handled is to get a friend to ring your company with an enquiry such as 'I need to order a part for a radio I bought from you some time ago. How do I go about it?' and see what happens.

Checklist

- Take the time to establish what it is the customer wants or who he needs to speak to.
- If your switchboard is too busy to always correctly route calls consider setting up a 'helpline' desk to handle enquiries for customers.
- When you get a call which has been misdirected, don't tell the customer he has come through to the wrong department!

- Ask open ended questions to gain as much information as you can.

- Check whether the customer has already spoken to someone in your organisation. Customers don't always volunteer information about previous conversations they may have had.

- Project a helpful and friendly attitude.

- The call may result in the need to check information. Explain this to your customer. Say how long you expect this to take and agree a convenient time to get back to the customer.

- If it is necessary to pass on the enquiry to someone else, give the caller the name and extension number of the person for future reference, but always check that your colleague rings the customer back if he is unable to accept the call immediately.

- Try to make your department a 'one stop' call for your customer.

- Have appropriate material easy to refer to on your desk, eg internal phone directory, company organisational chart, product lists and a message pad. (It helps to use brightly coloured message pads as this makes them easier to see on a desk.)

Complaints

The most common attitude in dealing with complaints is the tendency for the receiver of the call to take everything that is said personally. This can lead to conflict, if not confrontation. If a customer has rung in with a complaint, he has actually given you an opportunity to put things right. Usually customers simply take their business elsewhere. Listen with sympathy and understanding but don't be too quick to take the blame. Companies are frequently let down by staff who make comments such as 'We've had lots of similar complaints – I thought we'd sorted that out' or 'Yes, I'm afraid Mr Robinson does have a reputation for being rude' or worst of all 'I don't have anything to do with that side of our business'. Anybody who has ever had occasion to ring businesses with a complaint and has met with the response 'How did you get my name?' will recognise the feelings of frustration and anger which are fuelled by such an inane comment. The response should be not how the caller got the individual's name but what that individual is going to do to help the caller. It creates a very poor image of an organisation and indicates an unwillingness to help if not, indeed, personal paranoia. Remember the customer isn't always right – his perception of what is poor service or shoddy goods might be unrealistic. Customers may not have bothered to read their contracts properly and have unrealistic expectations of what the company can deliver in terms of after sales service. To establish whether the complaint is justified needs a patient listener but of course your staff do not have to be subjected to abuse, they should be trained to control the call.

The easiest way to regain control where customers are clearly losing their temper is to ask questions. Say 'Yes, I understand' but also verify whether they have raised this issue with you before. They may already be speaking to someone else on this matter. Customers can ring several people in the organisation with the same complaint if they think it will gain more attention. If you are not careful you can tie people up in a paper chase that can take a long time to unravel and whilst the customer may believe that he's raising merry hell and getting everybody to jump to attention, what he actually may be doing is adding further confusion and increasing the likelihood of his complaint not being dealt with properly. Once you have gathered the necessary information you need to move the call forward into negotiating a solution.

The simplest way to negotiate a solution is to ask the customer what they want. They may require only a small concession from you to bring the call to a satisfactory conclusion. If they have unrealistic expectations of what they believe to be a reasonable solution at least you have a starting point and you know what the extent of the problem is. Ask the customer if he's willing to look at alternatives. Say that you want to help him by resolving the problem. This is probably the most crucial part of the call and a plea must be made here for companies to recognise that you cannot control complaint calls and prevent them from escalating into major problems if you don't empower your employees to negotiate on your behalf. A framework needs to established which allows your employees to make decisions and understand the extent of their powers. If it is a situation that they cannot resolve, they need to be aware of how to progress to the next step.

If you have been asked to return a telephone call to a customer who has made a complaint, don't ask the customer to go over the same ground again. Start by confirming what you have been told and ask him to expand if necessary. And if the customer has rung you, always allow him to finish before trying to speak. Interruptions will only exacerbate the situation; the customer will think you are more interested in defending your company than in listening to him.

If the problem cannot be resolved immediately, tell the customer what you are going to do to bring the situation to a satisfactory conclusion and

33

if, as a manager, you get a request from an employee to become involved with a complaint at this stage, take the call. This demonstrates support for your employees and also a willingness to listen to what the customer is saying.

Checklist

- If his grievance is clear and justified say what you are going to do to rectify it immediately if you can.
- If it isn't straightforward, tell your customer you will get back to him once you have all the information you require. Thank him for bringing the matter to your attention and acknowledge that he has raised several points that need further investigation.
- Tell him you want to reach the right decision for both parties and you will need time to consider your action.
- If you agree to call him back at a particular time – *Stick to it*! Don't be late calling him – he will feel more aggrieved.
- When you reach a decision explain your reasoning. He is more likely to accept your decision, whatever it is, if he feels you have given the matter full consideration.
- Don't be too sympathetic. It may be more difficult to retract should you be unable to offer him the solution he wants. Offer empathy, not sympathy.
- If you are seeking a compromise, ask the customer what he wants. It's a starting point in a negotiation.
- If you do intend to change company procedures as a result of his call, thank him for giving you the opportunity to do so.
- Ask your customer if he is satisfied and reaffirm your wish to continue to do business with him.

Finance

INVOICE QUERIES

Nothing is more annoying for a customer than to be billed incorrectly. If these calls are dealt with by people who work in accounts or finance departments and who have no perceptible telephone skills, you have trouble. An off-hand response to a query exacerbates the situation and often results in the customer taking up a position where he refuses to pay any money at all, not just the disputed amount.

Avoid negative statements such as 'I'm sorry, we have a new computer and things are going wrong' or 'This has never happened before – it must be correct'. Rather seek to establish what the facts are and then tell the customer what solution you can offer. Always acknowledge that it is the customer who has been inconvenienced, not you by having a telephone call interrupt your normal working day.

CREDIT CONTROL

It is important to remain calm and professional at all times. Cajoling may be needed but don't lose sight of the fact that if your operator controls the call, she is far more likely to get a good result than if she ignores the structure of the call. Always gain agreement to mutual action. Either the customer is going to pay or you are going to have to proceed further with your collection process. Good telephone skills are essential for this type of call. It's a sensitive area – the customer may have made a genuine mistake or may be experiencing severe financial difficulties. Either way the call needs to be handled with care if you want to gain a mutually satisfactory outcome. The important thing is never to lose sight of the main objective, which is to effect some sort of agreement from your customer about when you can expect payment for the bill.

35

The sort of people in organisations who make these calls are vital to the profitability of your company. They are usually people who have chosen an administrative or non-customer-facing career. To be faced with one of the most direct customer confrontations possible can intimidate them and lead them into acting with hesitancy when approaching the main issue. Just as sales people can find it hard to ask for an order, credit collection people can find it hard to ask for money! However, this is precisely why they are making the call so the more time and attention you give to training them in these matters, the more effective your collections will be.

One managing director chose his telephone credit controller purely for her telephone skills. She was able to communicate easily and effectively with customers and reach a successful conclusion where those before her had failed. In this area, more than any other, good communication skills are necessary, coupled with a sense of purpose and a willingness to obtain a mutually satisfactory agreement. Try to avoid ending the call with vague promises to 'call you again next week, Mr Smith'.

Because people can be quite shy about asking for money many companies choose an alternative route by hiring independent collectors to work for them. If you take time to develop the skills of your people, there is no reason why your own employees should not be just as effective. Help them to understand that there is no shame in asking for money to settle a bill for goods or services which your company has provided. The customer ultimately recognises this and provided you approach the problem together, a satisfactory conclusion can be reached.

Handling internal and external calls

There is a marked difference in attitude towards internal and external calls taken or made by employees. Internal calls tend to be treated more casually. The caller is usually more relaxed and the receiver of the call often knows who it is on the other end of the line, therefore their communication tends to be freer. They worry less about how they sound or the interpretation that might be put on the information imparted. They can, depending of course on the relationship that each department has with another, dispense with formalities such as 'good morning' or 'how can I help you?' and get straight down to business. This can sometimes be useful. However it is just as important to extend common courtesies to one's business colleagues as it is to one's external customers.

Calls between internal customers and the way they are handled are just as important to a business as any other type of calls that are made. Your colleagues' perception of the way calls are handled will say as much about you as a manager as any other single thing. Failure to return calls when promised or provide information should be taken just as seriously as if it happened to an external customer. Internal calls help your business react quickly to external needs. If a colleague has a problem that he's trying to sort out, anything that you can do to help him to resolve this can only be of benefit to you and your organisation.

I've mentioned that internal calls usually encourage people to speak more freely than perhaps they otherwise would. With the development of new and ever more sophisticated telephone systems, it's a wise manager who points out some of the drawbacks to the people who use them. For example, if your staff are having a joke, check that the telephone loudspeaker isn't on or your customer could be sharing the fun. If you have a telephone system which displays the number of the person calling you, never fall into the trap of assuming that that is who is on the other end of the phone. Embarrassing mistakes can be made as it has been known for customers to borrow a phone to make a call. One manager found herself responding to a call with 'Hello ratbag!' thinking that she was addressing a colleague who was also a close friend. Unfortunately for her, the Managing Director had chosen to use the Personnel Manager's office to make some calls.

EXTERNAL CALLS

When making external calls a few simple guidelines apply. One is cost: it is cheaper to make an outgoing call after 1.00 pm than it is before. Therefore if you can save calls until the afternoon you are effectively helping your company to save money and reduce overheads. Of course this isn't always practical and certainly telephone sales teams would not be likely to apply this rule, since it would cut their working day by 50 per cent. New telephone business systems can now offer the facility of what is known as power dialling. This allows the telephone system to make outgoing calls which are only connected to an operator when the call is answered, thereby saving many hours where previously operators have wasted time waiting for the telephone to answered. This facility benefits anyone managing a high volume of outgoing calls.

37

It is extraordinary the lengths of time that callers are prepared to wait either for a phone to be answered or, once a connection is made, for that call to be transferred. If you've ever listened to a telephone call and timed the length of gap between speaking, it is not unusual to find that this can last for anything up to five minutes. Don't be prepared to hold on for so long, your time is too valuable, arrange to call back or leave a message. Managers may think that they are not wasting their time by holding because of course they can still be writing a memo or even conducting a conversation with someone else. However, telephone calls are expensive and it's much more effective to put the phone down and call back later. Whilst you are on the telephone you are also making yourself unavailable to others who may wish to contact you.

The 'after sales call'

For some customers major purchases are treated as 'one-off' decisions. Much time, effort and money is spent in attracting buyers into stores, showrooms or offices. Once the transaction is completed, the wheel is set in motion again to attract new business. Customers buy houses, cars, furniture, hi-fi equipment, seek advice then they leave your premises and never speak to you again.

Expensive catalogues and brochures are sometimes mailed but the return on this is low. Direct mail even to 'warm' prospects yields, on average, a two to three per cent response and the resulting sales may only be 20 per cent of this figure. Retailers have lost sales skills in their anxiety not to be too 'pushy' and the professions are reluctant to be seen to be too proactive in seeking further business. The danger is that the customer can interpret this passivity as a lack of interest.

When someone buys or sells a house, despite everything an agent may do to minimise the problems, it is a traumatic time for the customer. Unfortunately, the agent gets caught in the fallout. Once the dust has settled those memories dim and this is the time to talk to them. They will be surprised and flattered that you have called and this will go a long way to counteract any negative thoughts they may have had about your part in their house-moving experience. Of course, they are extremely unlikely to be needing your services immediately but you could benefit by being recommended to friends and relatives who may be about to enter the market.

The same can be said for other infrequent major purchases or the use of professional advice. Repeat business may be unrealistic in the short term but there is sometimes the opportunity for 'add on' business and the warm glow you give your customer will be reflected in his attitude towards you as a supplier. People like to share good experiences or be confident in their recommendations. The after sales call will, at the very least, help to cement your relationship with your customer and hopefully prompt him to recommend you to others.

The after sales call:
- Shows interest in your customer.
- May not have an immediate return.
- Could lead to recommendations.
- Could serve to identify further opportunities to do business.
- Leaves a warm glow.
- Cements the customer/supplier relationship.

Summary

Similar techniques can be used in all of the calls described above.

- Use the 'verbal handshake'.

- Introduce yourself clearly, say why you are calling and what the purpose of your call is.

- Let the receiver of the call know what you expect to gain from that call.

- Gather information using open-ended questions that are likely to draw out information from the person you are calling.

- Respond to information that is given and use it to determine how to develop the call further.

- Always acknowledge the information that you have been given.

- Say why you are asking the questions and what you hope to gain from it. Avoid asking superfluous questions, they do not progress the call.

- Gain agreement.

- Check your understanding. Make sure that you have drawn the right conclusion.

- Offer alternatives and allow your customer to choose.

- Negotiate a solution where possible.

- Close by thanking the customer for his time and for the opportunity to do business with him.

39

All the calls discussed in this chapter reflect different aspects of your relationship with your customer. Not all of them will be relevant to you but **some** will be. Once you have completed your telephone audit and identified the kind of calls you or your department are involved in, you can develop your training material to reflect the needs of your trainees.

Discuss with your staff the different aspects of each call and use these examples to stimulate further discussion.

Every call made from your organisation says as much about your company as any other area of activity can do.

In PR there is an adage: **it takes 30 years to build a reputation. One could add – it takes one telephone call to ruin it.**

3

Telephone skills

How to help your staff improve their technique

Introduction

Why does a ringing telephone induce a feeling of fear in many people? Their reluctance to answer is because they fear the unknown. Not knowing what the call is going to be about or indeed who will be on the other end of the phone, can produce a nervous reaction even in the most confident of people. For people who do not normally use the telephone in everyday business, this problem can be particularly difficult to overcome. If you are trying to introduce a culture where anybody may pick up the phone, you need to consider the ways in which you can help people build up confidence to help them overcome this fear. Surprisingly, senior managers can be particularly susceptible. One of the reasons is because they lack the comfort that the visual trappings of their success brings, for example a visitor to a senior manager's office may have the opportunity to be impressed by the manager's surroundings: it is impossible to convey this over the phone. Because of this they are thrown back on their own personal resources.

Managers may spend a great deal of time and effort polishing up presentation skills or writing skills: they must understand that as much effort needs to be given to telephone communication. Every businessman and business makes and receives telephone calls each day. You need to be sure that the messages you convey are the desired ones. For example, a director may take a telephone call and sound abrupt, uninterested and displeased at the interruption. The caller will perceive all these messages and a bad impression will be created. By paying attention to how they project themselves over the telephone, managers will find their image considerably enhanced.

Even the most senior managers in an organisation find telephone communication difficult. Either they don't treat it seriously enough, or worse, they assume that the same communication skills are required as in face to face contact. Nothing could be further from the truth.

> *'I haven't had training on the use of the phone specifically but it has been included, almost in passing, on communication courses I've attended.'*

> *'There has been an assumption that everybody can use the phone, therefore everyone knows how to make a phone call and knows how to react and respond. That attitude is changing and there is a greater awareness of the need for training.'*

Psychological factors which can inhibit telephone communication

CONFIDENCE BUILDING

41

> *'I must admit at first I thought – Oh, my God, I can't cope. In the end I took pride in being able to deal with the customers myself.'*

Building up confidence can be achieved by successful training, lots of experience and the opportunity to role play different situations. Training in all aspects of using the telephone will go a long way towards removing the nervousness that is very common. If situations arise where someone may pick up a telephone and take calls, perhaps for another manager, when they don't know how that department works or can't answer questions that may be put to them, it can have a serious effect on their confidence and this will be communicated to the caller.

Nervousness can demonstrate itself in one of two ways. The caller may find himself speaking to somebody with an over-hearty manner which is extremely off-putting if he is ringing up to complain. If he is ringing up to make a serious comment, someone giggling at the other end of the phone can be equally unwelcome. People can have nervous habits of which they are totally unaware and helping them to overcome these habits is best achieved by successful training. This training is not just in telephone skills and how to handle a call. It involves training in their own job and those of the people with whom they work. It is important to remember that any of your employees may at any time receive a call from an external source which will not be related to the department in which they work. A good example of this is when a marketing department may fully brief a sales department about a new campaign, or a mailing or TV advertisement, and fail to relate this information to other employees in the business. If your caller is responding to an advertisement on television, it doesn't say much for your company if the person to whom they are speaking knows absolutely nothing about it. If your employees take external calls, make sure they know what is happening in the business.

Help your people to build up their confidence by allowing them to discuss the problems they have when communicating over the telephone. Praise them for good calls and, when training needs are identified, introduce the appropriate training to counteract the difficulties as soon as possible.

SHYNESS

'It's in the hands of the user to choose how they want to sound and come across to the listener. For example, one can hide behind the telephone to put forward a very positive attitude when really one is quite nervous of who one is actually going to speak to.'

Remember that your staff may simply feel overwhelmed at giving the amount of consideration and time to their telephone techniques that you are asking them to give. This in turn will affect their ability to communicate effectively. Their natural inclination may be to hide from the problem. They may be effective communicators when talking to colleagues but not very good at presenting themselves to the public. You need to help them overcome this and the best way is to practise.

FAMILIARITY

If people are receiving similar types of calls, for example perhaps your people work in an order-taking department, the assumption can be made that each call is the same. Opportunities may be missed because the receiver of the call is failing to listen attentively enough to recognise the key differences in this particular call. Familiarity certainly does breed contempt. Repetitive outgoing calls, eg cold calling trap people into believing that the conversation will not present any new insights or freshness into the conversation. But remember – whilst they may have made this call many times before, your caller certainly hasn't received it. To him it is a totally new situation and an unusual thing. Therefore it is necessary to counteract the temptation not to pay as much attention to the call as you should.

ANXIETY

Probably the biggest barrier to making outgoing calls is that the caller is worried about what the person on the other end of the telephone is going to think. They spend so much time worrying about this that often they forget to listen. This failure to listen will lead to a breakdown in successful communication.

BOREDOM

'I rang a company for the first time yesterday and it was – "Yeah, who is it? Hold on a minute." – It was as if they had no interest.'

If you are bored, the ability to listen attentively will be impaired. Boredom can be transmitted over the telephone. If your caller feels you are uninterested in what they have to say, they will give up trying to make the effort.

- Knowledge of your business and good product training help people to deal with calls more confidently.
- Build up confidence by praising the positive aspects of the way the call was handled.
- Help your staff to overcome their inhibitions by encouraging them to practise using the telephone in different situations.
- Every call is different – even if you are dealing with repetitive calls, your customers are unique.
- A customer's impression when he rings you colours his whole attitude to your organisation.

Physical advantages and disadvantages of communicating by telephone

ADVANTAGES

'The phone is my main point of contact with branch managers. Conversations tend to be one to one with a manager so the use of

43

teleconferencing facilities are not appropriate. In my last position I used this facility a lot. I think they are tremendous. I used it a lot in the US but I think there is a hesitancy to do things like that here. In England you tend to drive somewhere or meet in the senior manager's office. It's a valuable tool. We need to change our attitude to the way we use the phone.

'I expect there are instances where I would rather be sitting with someone in a room because I could have shown something, but there again, I expect you can fax things to people. What I tend to do now is if I want people to see something I fax it and then say now pick up the telephone.

'A few years ago it was the case that you would prefer to have a face to face meeting but now I think this is unnecessary when you can fax documents. I feel quite comfortable using the phone.'

Because the telephone is such an intimate medium, it can lead to very close relationships between the caller and receiver of the call. This often surprises people. However, because all other psychological and physical barriers are removed, you are only using your voice to communicate and it's amazing how well people respond to this medium. One sales person I know knew the most intimate details about her customers. She was involved in selling retail advertising.

She knew when her customers were about to become fathers or mothers, when they celebrated anniversaries, where they went on holiday, what the VAT man was saying to them, indeed the free flow of conversation was such that she felt she should be able to recognise them should she pass them on the street. They felt that she was a friend, too. It was not unusual for her to receive boxes of chocolates or birthday cards. Yes, business was being conducted, but in such a friendly and informal way that a bond was being formed between the customer and the seller.

This degree of intimacy can almost never be achieved in a face to face situation where people are far more guarded about their true feelings. The important point here is to recognise that even though you may initially be inhibited by the fact that you cannot see the person to whom you are speaking, this can, in fact, be a tremendous advantage and if used well, can lead to a much more successful communication than a face to face situation may offer in certain circumstances.

The telephone makes everybody accessible. Every businessman – every customer – owns a telephone. Your company can enjoy the advantage of communicating with them without recourse to expensive letters or even more expensive meetings. There are no external visual factors to distract you from the call. It allows you to concentrate totally on what the speaker is saying to you.

The cost of a telephone call is much less than the cost of written communication (even though capital expenditure for telephone operations can be higher than that of dealing with customers by correspondence, telephones eventually pay for themselves in terms of efficiency and quality. This can help a company reduce overheads substantially, particularly if they find it necessary to remain in constant contact with customers. Another advantage, of course, is the immediacy of the telephone. Provided the person with whom you wish to speak is available, you can resolve situations immediately without having to wait for letters to be sent or received or for meetings to be arranged.

DISADVANTAGES

The major disadvantage of using the telephone is, of course, the lack of visual information. For example, you cannot tell if a conversation is going well. The encouraging smiles and nods are not available to give us any clues. It's difficult to establish if someone is nodding their head in agreement with what you say, or if indeed they are smiling. We cannot tell if the listener is giving us their full attention. Someone else may be in the room with them and may in fact be trying to conduct another conversation. A hand may be held over the receiver whilst this conversation is going on. Or worse, the person you are speaking to may be reading something or trying to attract the attention of a colleague or friend.

45

Because the communication between you is purely verbal, you may find it difficult to enforce agreements that have been reached (in a legal sense) or indeed to prove that such things were ever said when not supported by written documentation. For this reason a manager needs to establish what is reasonable and what is most effectively done by telephone.

HOW TO IMPROVE COMMUNICATION

Misunderstandings can be all too common when insufficient attention is paid to developing communication techniques when using the telephone. A call can also lack the warmth that a face to face meeting may generate. One of the ways to turn these disadvantages into advantages is to think about how we use our ears and our voices. Remember that the characteristics one may get away with in a face to face situation, for example a tendency to interrupt, can frequently be accepted when accompanied by a smile. However, on the telephone the person who is receiving the call cannot see that – it sounds plain rude to interrupt.

Listening – the key to a successful outcome

'The guy who is not good on the phone is the one who may know all the right things to ask but doesn't listen to the reply.'

People who communicate well on the telephone are not easily distracted. They don't respond to colleagues trying to interrupt their calls and they certainly don't respond to pieces of paper being put on their desk whilst they are conducting a conversation. The ability to concentrate totally on what the other person is saying is of paramount importance. One of the most frequent complaints of people who are obliged to use the telephone regularly in business is that their colleagues simply fail to appreciate how important it is not to distract someone who is on a telephone call. Whilst a noisy environment may be acceptable in that it indicates enthusiasm and liveliness, it does have to be remembered that it helps

enormously to keep background noise to a minimum to enable people on the phone to concentrate on what is being said to them. The key to good communication when using the telephone is to use your ears in twice the proportion that you use your mouth. No matter how charming, courteous and articulate your staff are, if they do not listen with full attention, vital information will be missed. Let the caller know you are listening by using phrases like 'Yes, I see' or 'I understand'. Demonstrate that you are actively listening otherwise they could think they are speaking into a void.

The voice

Because it is the instrument by which we convey our words, it is worth taking some time to consider how your staff use their voices on the telephone. Do they have forced, unnatural 'telephone voices'? Do you? Encourage your staff to relax and feel comfortable on the telephone.

Accents can be made to work for you provided that people take care to speak clearly – most people warm to someone who speaks with their own accent.

Projecting your personality

'One of the advantages is the fact that the other person, especially in business, conjures up all kinds of ideas of the type of person that you are. They gauge your moods and from that you can develop your own personality over the 'phone.'

A caller formulates images from what he hears, a speaker can only convey images via words and yet the communication process is more complex than this. After all, we know what the speaker looks like, don't we? How many times have you met someone you have spoken to on the telephone, only to find the reality totally at odds with the mental image of the speaker prior to the image?

A good way to demonstrate this is to play tapes of recorded voices to your staff. Ask them to describe their physical appearance – they always do. No-one challenges the impossibility of the task because as soon as the tapes play they immediately start to create mental images of the speaker. Interestingly, characteristics as well as physical appearances are also ascribed. 'He sounds a nice person.' 'He's obviously not a sales person.'

> *'We've all done it – talked to people and then met the person we've been talking to and had a real shock. Because when we've listened to people we've drawn our own mind's images of what we're expecting, be it a person, premises, the size of a business, and got there and been very surprised.'*

This exercise should clearly demonstrate a person's need to subject their telephone performance to closer scrutiny, with the objective of enhancing the more positive aspects of their voices when using the telephone.

BALANCING THE ADVANTAGES AND DISADVANTAGES

In a face to face situation a lot of physical clues are available for the visitor. The size and decor of an office give status clues, the physical appearance of the host conveys all sorts of messages about him – a smart dresser – ambition or pride, for example. The host is on his own territory and may be wary of invasion so the visitor will take some trouble to put him at ease. Courtesies are exchanged and pleasantries observed.

The potentially intimate nature of the telephone is particularly beneficial when trying to negotiate delicate situations such as complaints or disputes. Settlement is often easier to negotiate via the telephone as it removes the necessity of formalising offers in writing which can lead to entrenched positions. Verbal negotiation is far more satisfactory than written, simply because it is more flexible and responsive than written situations. Thus, a pleasant, friendly telephone call can arrest a problem before both sides become entrenched as letters start to fly.

Nuances can be more easily deflected, eg the tone of voice will indicate if someone is genuinely trying to reach a satisfactory conclusion or is simply being obstructive. Hesitations or objections can be voiced without being committed to a course of action simply because it has been confirmed in writing. Using the telephone implies a willingness to respond quickly to the requests of others. It demonstrates an ability to set aside whatever you are doing and to give the caller (or writer) your *full attention*.

House styles

The current fashion for using 'house styles' as a form of address to callers has mixed blessings. Certainly, a professional and welcoming response is desirable. However, it is possible to make the standard response so long that it generates impatience in the caller and the constant repetition of the phrase induces a catatonic, trance-like stare in the speaker. 'Good morning. Thank you for calling Bloggs & Company. Tracy speaking. How may I help you?' takes on all the verve of a mantra! If this response is given to all callers, including other employees, the level of impatience rises in proportion to the number of times it is heard. Far more important than the format of the response is the *way* in which it is spoken. Forcing people into a scripted straitjacket does not promote sincerity or enthusiasm. However, it is wise to stick to a few general rules:

- If the call is at the switchboard, offer 'Good morning' or 'Good afternoon', followed by the company name. The caller may not hear the first word on connection so if you start with the company he may not hear it correctly.
- If the call is being re-directed internally, offer 'Good morning/ afternoon' followed by the name of the department.
- Whilst the offer of a name is desirable, it doesn't necessarily have to be in the opening address. It is acceptable to offer it early in the conversation and invite the caller to make a note of it.
- Keep it short and simple.

KNOW YOUR TELEPHONE SYSTEM

Whether your system is simple or sophisticated, ensure your staff know how to use it to its full advantage. They should be familiar with the following features:

- How to get an external line.
- How to re-route calls.
- How to put the caller on hold.
- How to use DDI lines.
- How to use last number redial, memory and conference features.

If your staff are encouraged to use ansaphones, do check that they appreciate the features of the system. In one company, for example, managers who were often away for two or three days at a time left ansaphones on. The company totally failed to take account of the problem that people who left messages frequently found that their calls weren't answered until the managers came back. The managers concerned did have the facility to dial their telephones and pick up messages from the system. Unfortunately they either didn't know how, or failed to do so. The result was that when the tapes were played, people who had rung in asking for calls to be returned usually after the second or third day of total unresponsiveness were not asking in quite the same polite was as they did originally.

49

If at all possible, arrange for somebody to cover for an unattended line or extension. That way your company is always available to your customers. If you are a small organisation and you simply don't have the staff or the telephone systems to make this possible, then often an ansaphone is the only way. However, if you do use one, make sure you listen to the messages frequently, otherwise you create more problems when in actual fact you were hoping to solve them!

Paint the picture, tell the story – how words create mental pictures

An ill-judged choice of words can lead to many misunderstandings and can convey totally the wrong impression. For example, consider the difference between 'You've been put through to the wrong department', 'You've come through to the wrong department' and 'We've put you through to the wrong department'. Each sentence conveys just a slightly different shade of meaning and succeeds in putting the blame on a different party, that is the switchboard, the customer or the company. The choice of words and tone in which they are conveyed are crucial to the successful outcome of any call. Because you only have words to create a mental picture, some time should be devoted to developing word skills. This doesn't necessarily mean an improved vocabulary, although a good vocabulary is obviously desirable. It is more important to be able to select the right emotive words to describe a product or situation. This has often been called 'selling the sizzle, not the sausage'. That is, a pan of sizzling sausages creates a far more appealing picture than a simple description of a packet of sausages wrapped in polythene. (Vegetarians might like to apply this principle to warmth v. blanket or sparkle v. diamond.)

It's not what you say, it's the way that you say it

A good way to demonstrate this point to your employees is to make a transcript of a real live call, or role play. Take out identifying factors such as names, either of the caller or the customer. Have it typed up and distribute copies to your staff in your next training session. Invite them to read the transcript in different tones of voice. You will be surprised how this alters the meaning conveyed. In one transcript taken in just such a situation, the employee referred to her company as being 'rubbish'. This response was in answer to an accusation made by the customer that her company was indeed 'rubbish'. On paper it looked absolutely appalling and indeed in any circumstances this could not be considered a wise response. However, the way in which the word was said by the employee was lighthearted and certainly not intended to convey that she truly believed that this was the case.

50

Consider the following:

'Doctor is busy. Can you tell me what it's about?'

Patients' tales of battles with a surgery receptionist are legendary, yet most receptionists will defend themselves by saying that they are only trying to help. So why the misconception? Too often efficiency is perceived as cold and uninterested. This telephone manner is very common in business situations, yet goes unchallenged as customers simply take their business elsewhere. It's more difficult to change doctors.

How can you avoid this situation? It's very simple.

- Every time you ask for information explain why you need it.
- Say why someone is unavailable and what you can do to help.

This will eliminate the interrogatory style of questioning and will achieve better results as it reassures the caller that you do genuinely want to help. In business, employees may need to establish facts to progress a call but they must never lose sight of the fact that without explanations a caller can only interpret questions as obstructive.

Questioning techniques

Skilled questioning will elicit information in a conversational way. The use of open-ended questions will encourage the speaker to expand his answers, often providing extra information pertinent to the situation. Open-ended questions begin with the words *Who, What, Where, Which, Why and How*. The use of close-ended questions helps to confirm what has already been said or to gain agreement. They also help you to control the conversation. Close-ended questions start with *Would, Could, Should, Do, Did, Are, Can, Has, Have* etc. However, whilst close-ended questions can keep wafflers under control, they should be used sparingly as they can turn a conversation into an interrogation.

51

A good way to help your staff to develop questioning techniques is to ask your staff to imagine that they are only allowed to ask three questions. You can set them the challenge of trying to find out as much about the other person as possible. This will help develop word and questioning skills.

The most skilled questioners are the ones likely to speak least on the telephone. All they will use is the occasional interjection of a 'Yes' or 'I see' on the phone because the question they've asked in the first place has been such that it has managed to extract a lot of information from a fairly short question. To develop skilled questioning techniques you first need to establish what sort of information it is you're asking for. Too often the temptation is to try to extract more information than is actually needed to complete the call successfully. Remember there is always the time limitation on the telephone. Whilst in a meeting you may have up to an hour to conduct a conversation, an average telephone call will only last three or four minutes at most. Therefore the time you spend on the telephone has to be meaningful and every second is important.

I'm not going to suggest specific questions because your staff need to develop their own. They need to develop their own style, too. Forcing people into script situations doesn't allow them to grow as good telephone communicators.

A good telephone technique is to ask the person to whom you are speaking what they think about something or ask them to volunteer an opinion. This has the advantage of extracting a lot of information but only through asking one or two questions. For example, think of the sort of response you would get to the question 'Do you like our products?' and then think of the sort of response you might get to the question 'What do you think about our new products?' With luck the second question will not only give you valuable information about what the customer thinks about the product, he will probably also draw comparisons with products he may already be using.

Some useful exercises

- Listen to tapes of other colleagues – paint a word picture of them.
- Experiment with questions – find the ones you are comfortable with.
- Ask a member of a group to describe a complex object to others. Ask them to draw it. Don't allow questions from the group. When finished, compare the results. (A good 'listening' exercise, this also helps to develop the describer's ability to paint word pictures.)
- After training ask your staff to list ways in which they would now handle a call differently.
- Ask your staff to demonstrate key features of your phone system.
- Tell your staff you will call them (or nominate a colleague and complete a call analysis sheet (Fig. 3.1)).

CALL ANALYSIS SHEET

	Poor	Satisfactory	Good	Exc.
Introduction				
Knowledge of phone system				
Knowledge of co.-personnel				
Knowledge of dept. responsibilities				
Control of call				
Offered solution				
Agreed action				
Checked caller's name				
Used name				
Prompt answer				
Listened carefully				
Message pad and pen available				
Offered own name and tel. ext.				
Offered alternative name and tel. (if likely to be unavailable)				

53

Fig 3.1 Call analysis sheet

4

Training for success and profit

Introduction

'As you become more senior it is expected that you know how to use the 'phone. If you present yourself well at other times, then it is assumed you must be okay on the 'phone.'

Constant training and monitoring of performance is essential to the success of any telephone user in an organisation. Helping your employees use the full potential of any telephone situation will enhance their job performance and, if done well, will increase their contribution to your department's performance and profitability.

'Across the board everybody is on the 'phone. The secretaries, assistants, trainees, partners – everybody in the firm has to use the 'phone so it is really important that they all have a good understanding of it.'

The opportunities for imaginative training sessions on using the telephone are much more plentiful than in most training situations in the workplace. It should be fun for all parties and can be very motivating if done correctly. Constant use of the telephone can lead to bad habits, and boredom constantly threatens. The only stimulus is often what is being said at the other end of the 'phone, or what is happening in the office. Training can go a long way to counteract this.

Your employees' conversations with customers should be constantly monitored, and ways to improve them should be recognised and communicated. A structured approach is essential, with long-term objectives as well as immediate needs being addressed. *Ad-hoc*, spontaneous training sessions don't give confidence to the trainee, but reinforce the belief that it's unnecessary, especially amongst experienced staff. They must be aware that you wish to achieve specific objectives, and these must be communicated to them. Essential to this process is commitment to the development and enhancement of your employees' knowledge of your company and its products or services. The more they know, the more effectively they can communicate with your customers.

Ask your managing director to discuss your company's prospects for the future, or your marketing director to discuss competitor activities. These discussions can lead to a heated debate but are tremendous for giving your staff a feeling of involvement in your company's activities. It also greatly improves inter-departmental relationships.

How to use training to counteract boredom arising from repetitive activity

A good training session should leave your employees feeling on a high and keen to get back to the job to put all those good ideas you've given them into practice. Where your employees are engaged in telephone contact work which is repetitive – perhaps they are order takers or they have to make cold calls to arrange appointments, only training can alert them to spot what is different in each telephone call. Good training requires a strong commitment from you to ensure that the training is fresh. You need to be constantly creative, looking for new ways to present similar material. You should constantly revise the training material that you use. Poor training will only produce the response from employees – 'Oh no, not another training session!'. The important thing is to use training not only to involve your team and help them to examine their own abilities but also to help them create new ideas and new ways of doing the same job which will increase their effectiveness on the telephone. By involving the team, their level of commitment to a good outcome from the training session will be increased. Nothing is worse than a trainer doing all the talking. Without that involvement from the team, all your efforts will be wasted.

55

Keeping it fresh, keeping it relevant

A good way to keep your telephone training fresh is to find out for yourself what kind of calls your people are taking or indeed making. Spend time on the telephone. Talk to your customers. Listen to the sort of enquiries your people may be dealing with. By making these calls yourself you will develop a keen ear for the relevant issues. To create interesting role plays, you need to have first hand, up to date knowledge of the types of situation your people are likely to face. Remember it is neither necessary, nor indeed desirable, for you to do all the training yourself. A good way to create an interesting training session is to involve other people in the company, or members of your own department or members of a telecontact team. Ask them to do presentations on different aspects of the calls that they handle.

Empowerment through personal development

One of the major problems for a manager when training people to handle enquiries is that too often they forget that for employees to be as effective as they can be, they need to have a degree of control over the outcome of the call. It is wasting everybody's time if they need to refer upwards for every kind of decision. Allow people to handle the call through to its conclusion in their own way. The person on the telephone is best placed to make a decision. An example of this might be where a customer has rung in to make a complaint. If your employees have the ability to make a decision as to whether the customer has a valid point or not, and if so, what action will be taken to redeem the situation, it will drastically reduce the amount of times that irate customers are coming through to you because they have failed to be dealt with satisfactorily.

Knowledge of your company, its limitations and its possibilities, enables your telecontact team to come up with solutions without referring to anyone else. By empowering your employees to make these decisions they can act with impressive and speedy response to situations they face on the telephone. Even where they may need to refer upwards to provide a solution, they can still get back to your prospects or customers the same day. With field sales this process can often take weeks and it doesn't imply a speedy response to a customer's enquiry.

If you have reservations about your employees' ability to do this, then the management issue must be how to help them reach the point where they have confidence in their ability to analyse problem situations. Personal development plans can help you achieve this.

A personal development plan is not a training plan – it's about developing your people. Perhaps they could write a training module for you or investigate an issue that is causing concern. They could find out how communication works throughout the company and give ideas and suggestions as to how your department fits into that overall picture. By giving them the opportunity to make 'small' decisions, you will help them along the path to making quite significant decisions with confidence. The more empowerment you give your employees on the telephone, the less likely you are to become involved in situations which have escalated beyond the point of agreement between your employee and a customer.

Planning, developing and delivering effective telephone training

First of all, decide what your objectives are. Is it to help employees answer general enquiries which they may be required to help with? Is it to sell, to order take, to account manage? Perhaps you are considering an induction course for new employees. Or perhaps you already have people whose telephone skills you wish to develop. Remember their training needs will be different.

Developing telephone training in a business requires a lot of imagination on the part of the manager. It does help to talk to people who have been there before you. For example, if you work for a large organisation that has its own telephone sales or telemarketing department, talk to their managers and ask them for their ideas. Talk to managers in the business about the sorts of skills they believe your people should have. What will help them when they ring your department? Is it knowledge of the business? Is it the ability to make decisions? Too often telephone training is confined to pure technique – in other words how your employee handles the telephone call – but remember that in order for them to be effective in this they need to be supported by all kinds of other training as well, particularly knowledge about your company and its products or services.

Your training plan should start off by incorporating all the things that your employees absolutely need to know. The standards you require – eg a call must be answered within three rings. How to answer the telephone call, what the company's corporate response is, whom to talk to if they run into problems. This can probably be achieved in a fairly short space of time, but remember that you are also going to use training to counteract the boredom and repetition that will set in later on. To do this, you should look at developing a training plan that will cover a period of say 12 months. Look at the things you need to achieve immediately and then bolt on training modules that can be run throughout the year. Your training plan should include the following:

Telephone techniques, communicating over the phone and the difference between this and face to face communication. How to project personality. The choice and use of words. The standards that you require and product knowledge. If your training plan is for sales people, obviously you will then have to incorporate all the sales skills necessary to help your people achieve a sale over the telephone. Thus they need to be aware of the structured approach to telephone selling and of course the customer's buying process. Finally they need to understand the systems within your own organisation in order either to process an order, or to book an appointment.

Effective telephone training can only be delivered by an enthusiastic and committed trainer. If you yourself are half-hearted about the training session, imagine the reaction of your employees. If you feel that you do not have the requisite skills to deliver good telephone training, you need to identify someone in your organisation who has, and gain their co-operation.

Techniques for creating interesting modules

The key to creating interesting training sessions is variety. You can introduce variety initially by the method of training chosen and there-after by the material that you use. Let us consider some of the methods that may be available to you. One to one training, classroom sessions, group sessions and side by side. Then consider the material that you are going to use. This could be role plays, scripts or even recordings.

ONE TO ONE

This training method is ideally used where perhaps you have a new employee who still needs to have confidence building sessions. One to one can be used to discuss problems that your employee may be having. Criticism is far more acceptable when it is delivered in privacy. Group sessions are never an acceptable forum for personal criticism and, worse, can lead to members of the group voicing their criticisms so that newer members of a group can feel overwhelmed by so many negative comments. However, for prolonged training sessions one to one training is not recommended as you will soon begin to tire of each other's voice.

CLASSROOM SESSIONS

These are particularly effective when you need to train a large number of people at the same time. However, to be practical you cannot really hope to have an effective session if you have more than ten people in the group as it will not allow you sufficient opportunity to listen to feedback from the group and to give adequate individual attention. A classroom session can further be made interesting by use of overheads, flipcharts and video. Classroom sessions are usually most effective when used as part of your team meeting programme. Every team meeting should have a training element in it – training is motivational and you want to motivate your staff at a team meeting.

GROUP SESSIONS

Group sessions are probably the most energetic training sessions. Here everybody will be expected to take part. Role plays should be carried out with every member of the group taking it in turns to act as customer and employee.

SIDE BY SIDE TRAINING

Side by side training is very useful when you wish to find out more about how your employee conducts him/herself on the telephone. By being in such close proximity, you will also be able to identify time management issues, or indeed organisational ones. Do they have to hand everything necessary for them to achieve a good result? Are customer records in pristine condition? Do employees fully understand the keyboard which they may be using? Do they have the appropriate sales manual available? Do they have mailshots that your company is sending out easily accessible and in a usable format for reference during the call? If they are involved in handling enquiries, do they have the appropriate telephone directory? Is it up to date? Are the training manuals in good order? All these things can be checked in a side by side situation, as well of course as listening to how the call develops.

What follows are some useful ideas to help you develop interesting training material. Use tape recorders extensively. They can be tremendously beneficial especially as they alone help to create the sort of environment in which you are seeking to improve communication – ie without visual clues. Whilst videos can be useful to demonstrate certain techniques, nothing is quite as real as listening to a tape recorder. For example, somebody may be kept waiting on hold for up to five minutes. Record this silence. Simulate the telephone call and include in it the actual amount of time that somebody has been kept waiting. This is a very powerful demonstration to your employees of what it must be like to be left hanging on the other end of a telephone.

Ask your employees to tape their own voices and to offer a critical analysis. Do they sound on tape the way they believe they sound on the telephone? Naturally, people very rarely do recognise the way they sound on tape. It's shocking the first time but as they become more experienced, they will recognise the value of tape analysis. Perhaps they have mannerisms, repeating certain words for example, which they use constantly in conversation without realising they are doing so. On the telephone this can be an extremely irritating habit and needs to be addressed. Perhaps they think they are fluent in product knowledge but find when they record themselves that they sound flustered and unsure of how to answer a question.

Tape recordings, as no other method, can really demonstrate at first hand the areas in which your staff need to make improvements. In this training session you will be required to do little more than direct the flow of conversation. People find it easy to comment on tape recordings and will volunteer their faults before you need to do so. This essentially is what you're seeking to achieve. People will only recognise faults and do something about them if they are readily able to identify faults for themselves. Self analysis should always be encouraged as it is the shortest route to improvement.

Finally one manager I know used the tape recorder very creatively. He interviewed some of his customers, asking them to discuss what they liked about a call and what they disliked. One customer revealed on tape that he was very happy to take calls from people if he felt they had an interesting proposition. For example, if a caller was offering a way to improve distribution problems and he was currently considering the same thing, he would be very interested in taking the call. This underlined to this manager's employees just how confident they ought to feel when they've got through to somebody. Just by taking the call the customer is demonstrating a willingness to listen. The manager also asked customers to comment on how calls to their business were handled and this provided further insight for the team into the customer's viewpoint.

Using tape recordings also helps your team improve their listening skills. They have to concentrate very hard on what is being said on the tape, which is exactly what you want to achieve.

All organisations are now finding themselves working in an increasingly pressured environment. Your staff may be feeling some of these pressures but of course the thing you want to do is to help them convey the positive aspects of your company over the telephone. So, invite colleagues in, ask them to talk about various aspects of the business which may be of interest to your department. If you work in an accounts department, involve sales managers. If you work in sales, get somebody from the operational side of the business to talk to your people. This not only increases product knowledge but develops a sense of involvement throughout the company and will certainly further better communication between departments.

61

Quizzes are a very useful training tool. Why not start off your training session with a buzz test. This could cover perhaps 20 or 30 references to issues on which you want to train your people – knowledge of the company, knowledge of product or services and so forth. A lot of fun can be had with quizzes and you will be amazed at how competitive people will be. You can award a small token prize for whoever scores the highest mark. It is also a very good way to test understanding of subjects that you may have covered.

ROLE PLAYS

Role plays are a key element for developing your staff's telephone skills. The role play can be done within a classroom environment extracting two volunteers from the group – one to act as a customer and one as a member of the company. After briefing both parties as to how the call should be handled, you can invite the rest of the group to make comments on various aspects of the call. Was it opened in the right way? Did the caller offer a name? And so on. You can either ask the group to observe the whole call or delegate each member of the group to observe one particular aspect of the call. Again, you are constantly seeking ways of conducting similar training sessions using slightly different techniques to create and maintain interest. The person who has observed the role play can produce an assessment sheet (see Fig. 4.1). As a follow on from this, a training report may be written up with the trainee. Fig. 4.2 gives a sample report.

The involvement of members of your team in these sessions can be very productive. By asking them to do presentations, you also create an environment whereby your team members will seek to outdo each other. People can be extremely competitive in situations like this and you will probably find that, with imagination on the part of your team, the material used for the presentations, for example illustrated acetates to illustrate a certain viewpoint, will add to the training material you've already got. I can certainly remember one particular acetate which displayed a clock that had 65 hours on it – the point being that there were never enough hours in the day and even with a 65 hour clock you still wouldn't have enough time to do everything. This clock amused everybody and was used by every other manager in the organisation when conducting time management courses. By allowing the free flow of information between departments, you can pick up ideas and schemes to enable your training sessions to be just that little bit more interesting.

Informed staff means informed customers

If your staff are in a position where they take calls externally, ie they are talking to your customers, it is very important to ensure that they are aware of what your company is up to. It is not unusual for a marketing or PR department to organise a whole campaign and then fail to brief their own employees.

If your company is prone to this sort of poor communication, you need to make it your responsibility to make sure your staff are fully briefed. If memos wing their way towards you, don't let them gather dust on your desk. Read them and see if there is anything in there that will help your people to do their job better. If there is, make sure that they get the opportunity to see it. You can also consider communication by your own normal company channels. You may have a newspaper or a news bulletin which is circulated to your team. Whatever it is, try to ensure that your department is featured in this. If every manager did this in an organisation, your staff would soon be fully informed as to what the rest of the organisation was doing.

The larger the organisation, the more prone it is to break itself down into

ASSESSMENT SHEET – ROLE PLAYS

Role play no:

	Comments	A	B	C
Introduction/establish rapport with customer				
Information gathering/use of open and close ended questions				
Identified a business opportunity and linked to a proposition				
Discussed benefits to customer of proposition				
Gained commitment from customer/closed call				
Ability to handle objections				

A = Needs further discussion

B = Satisfactory

C = Satisfactory +

* Tick score box to indicate skill level

* You can substitute key areas as appropriate to the nature of a call

Fig. 4.1 Assessment sheet – role plays

TRAINING REPORT

Trainee: _____   Trainer: _____

Date: _____

No. of calls made		Type of calls	

Training given:

* Classroom		Tape analysis		Role play		*

* Categorise type of training you are most likely to give.

**			

** List of areas you are most likely to train on.

Comments:

Next training date:	Subject:

Fig. 4.2 Training reports

little cliques. The problem with this is that sometimes the right hand doesn't know what the left hand is doing. If internal customers are muddled, imagine how your external customers feel when they contact you. If you see articles or features in the press about your company or the area of industry or service in which it operates, cut them out and distribute them amongst your staff. Maintain a high level of interest in your company and what it is doing. You may find there are snippets of information that could be circulated from internal sources. If the sales department has had a record month, surely this is a matter of good news for everybody in the organisation, not just in sales. If you are responsible for collecting revenue for the company and you have a particularly good month, you should ensure that your department's reputation is grown throughout the organisation as well. This is not self-aggrandisement, it is enabling your employees to be fully informed about the company and where it is going. It encourages pride in a company that employees can then communicate to customers.

Remember that communication is a two way process. The more you communicate with your fellow managers, the more likely they are to communicate changes within the organisation to you. This should help all concerned to ensure that the message given to the customer is the right one. Keeping your staff informed means not just talking about your own company, but about your competitors as well. Make sure that they are kept up to date with developments in the market place.

One of your objectives in keeping your staff informed is to ensure uniform standards. A very effective way of achieving this is to introduce an operating manual into your department. The operating manual should set out the standards that you require. For example, if you require the telephone to be answered within three rings, this should be clearly stated. If you have a corporate form of address, indicate that this should always be used. The operating manual will help your employees be effective on the telephone. The following is a list of some of the things you may wish to include in your operating manual.

- Telephone standards required – eg number of rings and corporate response.
- Organisational charts.
- Telephone numbers.
- Key points about products or services on offer.
- Suggested action procedures for employees to follow when your staff are answering enquiries.

It should be a 'how to' manual – how to take an order, how to make an account management call, how to deal with an enquiry, and so forth. By clearly setting out these standards your employees should achieve a good level of understanding of what you, as a manager, expect from them when they talk to customers on the telephone. The operating manual should be flexible and allow you to change material as your own company changes. For example, changes of address, location or whatever.

How to write telephone training material

Any manager who has ever sat down and tried to write a role play will know just how frustrating this can be. Good role plays are the key to successful role play in training sessions. One of the major difficulties with role plays is that people somehow don't feel comfortable doing them because it isn't a real situation. Time and again you hear people say 'I wouldn't have said that in a real situation'. Bad role plays lead to stilted training sessions and can be a switch off for your employees. By simply going round and talking to sales people within the business or even members of your own team, you will soon have all the true life situations that you could hope for. Use the role play guide that is printed in this book. This should prompt you to ask the right sort of questions thus enabling you to come up with a useful scenario. You can also help your staff develop word skills by writing out lists of emotive statements. For example, you could ask them to examine the difference between calling to 'book an appointment' and calling to 'arrange a meeting'.

Transcripts can be made from live recorded calls and are particularly useful for demonstrating training points. They are all the more effective when you include everything good and bad that is said. If callers are kept on hold, indicate when this happens and how long the caller is kept waiting. Remove all identifying pointers such as the name of the customer and the person who took the call. This allows for a freer expression from your team about what they think happened in the call.

Extract particularly illustrative random points from the call and use overheads to let the team consider the comment. If you transcribe the full call you can choose two members of the team to read the transcript as they would a radio script. When it is finished ask the participants to say how they felt as the caller and the customer. Then invite comments from the group.

CALL TRANSCRIPT

CUSTOMER: Can you post it to me tonight?!

EMPLOYEE: Theoretically it should leave tonight, first class post. That's what should happen – whether it will do in practice or not remains to be seen, but I'll certainly make the request for you.

Analysis

- Start by asking your group to interpret what the speaker meant to say, and how it could be interpreted by the person being spoken to.
- Invite comments on the choice of words and how they contribute to the meaning conveyed. Clearly, this is an example of the speaker not accepting responsibility for ensuring the customer receives his goods in the post the following day.
- It also manages to imply to the customer that such a simple task is beyond the wit and resources of this department. If this employee's company hopes to do business with this customer, they first need to convince their employee that they can do so!

67

Background

It may seem unfair to take a paragraph out of context, but this is exactly what listeners do. Only about 50 per cent of any telephone conversation is retained by the listener, hence the need for constant repetition of a sales message to a target audience. You can be sure that negative comments like this will be remembered so use random phrases to underline and drive home a point.

When this comment was shown to a group of people, the person who made the comment failed to recognise himself as the speaker and was as critical as his colleagues in upbraiding the speaker. Shocked when informed that it was him (in a one to one situation) he vowed to be more careful about his choice of words in future.

Managers should be aware that gaffes like this constantly happen in any business. Never assume that, because you have trained them on presenting a positive image, it will automatically follow for your employees to do this every time. When a group is given the chance to analyse real conversations, the points learned stay with them longer.

Criticism is all the more effective when given by one's peers, and that –
more than anything – will drive home the manager's message.

CALL TRANSCRIPT

Phone answered in two rings.

EMPLOYEE: Good afternoon, XXXX Leasing. Can I help you?

CALLER: Oh, good afternoon. I wonder if you can help me. I am
looking for a lease vehicle.

EMPLOYEE: Yes, just a minute. I'll find out what number you should ring.
(Caller put on hold.)
Hello. If you ring. (Gives number.) Okay then?

CALLER: Yes, thank you.

(Both say) 'Bye'

(Caller then rings telephone number she has been given.)

CALLER: Oh, good afternoon. I want to lease a car please.

EMPLOYEE: Oh, er . . . do you belong to a limited company?

CALLER: Yes, it's XXXXXX Ltd.

EMPLOYEE: Oh, right. One minute, I'll put you through to (*voice trails off
– impossible to hear*).

*(Caller is put through. Whoever answers the phone cannot be heard at
first so the name is unclear.)*

CALLER: Oh, hello. I would like some quotes on leasing please.

EMPLOYEE: Right, fine. Are you an existing customer?

CALLER: No, I'm not.

EMPLOYEE: Okey Dokey. Sorry, we're usually told beforehand when
someone is coming through. Right. Well, er, are you a
limited company?

CALLER: Yes, we are.

EMPLOYEE: And you've been in business more than a year?

CALLER: Yes, we have.

EMPLOYEE: How many vehicles have you?

CALLER: We have eight in total.

EMPLOYEE: Oh no. This isn't working. Hang on, I'll just get a pen. (*Customer left on hold.*) Right. What is the name of your company? (*Caller gives name and address. No attempt is made to check the address.*) Lovely. And your name? (*Caller gives first name.*) What's your surname?

CALLER: Oh, sorry. (*Gives name.*)

EMPLOYEE: You don't mind answering these questions?

CALLER: No, not at all.

EMPLOYEE: Er, a little bit more businesslike as the saying goes! Er, what is the telephone number? (*Caller gives telephone number.*) And what's your position in the company?

CALLER: I'm secretary to the Financial Director.

69

EMPLOYEE: (*Silence.*) So, he's the decision maker, is he?

CALLER: Yes, he is. He's the one who decides what we are going to do – whether to buy a vehicle or to contract hire.

EMPLOYEE: What kind of business is it?

CALLER: We are an engineering firm.

EMPLOYEE: Lovely. And you've only got about eight at the moment?

CALLER: Yes, that's right, but I'm just looking for one at the moment.

EMPLOYEE: That's fine. Are they executive or commercial?

CALLER: Oh, well it's for a rep. actually.

EMPLOYEE: I mean the ones you've got at the moment. Are they executive or commercial?

CALLER: I'm sorry, how do you mean?

EMPLOYEE: Oh, I think cars.

CALLER: Oh, I see. They are all cars.

EMPLOYEE: Do you purchase them?

CALLER: Well it depends on the circumstances really. Some are on finance lease, some are on contract hire, but this one we are looking to contract hire.

EMPLOYEE: Oh, right. What other companies do you contract them from?

CALLER: Well it varies, really. I mean I don't get involved in that decision. That's down to the FD.

EMPLOYEE: Okey Dokey. And what type of vehicle would you like me to quote for?

CALLER: A Sierra please. (*Gives details of car.*)

EMPLOYEE: Is it a manual?

CALLER: Yes.

EMPLOYEE: Anything else?

CALLER: No, that is the one we are looking at at the moment.

EMPLOYEE: Do you want any extras? Metallic paint or anything?

CALLER: Er, no. I think it's just the standard car.

EMPLOYEE: And his mileage?

CALLER: It's just average. I don't know.

EMPLOYEE: How many years?

CALLER: Er, three years.

EMPLOYEE: About 20,0000?

CALLER: Yes, fine.

EMPLOYEE: Okay then. Maintenance?

CALLER: Yes.

EMPLOYEE: We could do it without as well if you want.

CALLER: Yes please, with and without.

EMPLOYEE: Which do you want, 24, immediate or 48?

CALLER: 24 please – (*pause*) – can you give me a quote now, over the phone, just so that I can put it to him before I go this afternoon?

EMPLOYEE: Yes, I'd love to and I'll fax it over to you after I've done it. What's the fax number?

CALLER: Sorry, we're not on the fax.

EMPLOYEE: Oh! Er I suppose I could post it to you.

CALLER: Yes, that's fine.

EMPLOYEE: Right. Now, what is the date today? It's the 21st tomorrow, thank God that's Saturday. I hate boring old work! How did you find out about us?

CALLER: YP.

EMPLOYEE: Oh, yeah, that's a regular one. (*Silence.*)

CALLER: Okay?

EMPLOYEE: Oh . . . er last question. How do you want to pay. A normal one of three pay two?

CALLER: We want to pay three months up front with the last two months of the contract free.

EMPLOYEE: Oh, you're such an easy customer to deal with. You know all the questions before I say them.

CALLER: Okay. So would you put the quote in the post for me please?

EMPLOYEE: I'd love to.

CALLER: That's great. Thanks.

EMPLOYEE: You're sure you don't want me to quote on different mileages?

CALLER: No, that's fine.

EMPLOYEE: All right then.

CALLER: Thanks.

(*Both together*) Bye.

Analysis

- The first call leaves the customer with the choice of ringing the alternative number she has been given. If she chooses not to do so, a business opportunity would have been lost.

71

- Questions are asked which appear unrelated to the flow of conversation.

- The use of slang does not give a professional image.

- The customer is not asked if she minds being put on hold. The employee speaks to herself as if the customer is not there.

- 'A little bit more businesslike . . .' Obviously someone has attempted to improve the employee's standards but the message still hasn't been received.

- 'Decision makers' should exist only in sales training manuals.

- Jargon is meaningless to your customers. 'Executive or Commercial'.

- A guess is made at the customer's contract requirements. What is average for the business may not be average for the customer.

- The Friday afternoon syndrome! Your employees need to be as fresh and enthusiastic on Friday as they are on Monday.

- The employee obviously feels self-conscious about the questions she has to ask.

- The quote is going out but the company has no real idea of what the customer actually needs.

- The customer's name is not used once.

Background

The company (a well-known national one) was picked out of Yellow Pages. The telephone number was an incorrect one for sales enquiries. The company must have had similar calls before but no attempt has been made to redirect telephone calls in a more positive and welcoming way.

The customer was 'easy'. Your customers may not be. The employee sounded friendly but this was negated by a sloppy approach to the information gathering part of the call. Its unstructured approach, use of slang and company jargon were all negative aspects presented to the caller.

No attempt was made to suggest ringing the customer back with a price. The alternative chosen was the post, despite the fact that the customer indicated she would like to give some details to her manager the same day.

The silences which can occur when an employee is writing responses down demonstrates a concern for the company to record marketing information rather than a willingness to listen to a customer's replies.

If your caller is gathering information for someone else, always establish the name of that person for future reference. Where possible, try to speak to him yourself. Why pass on messages if it is possible to speak directly to your customers?

CALL TRANSCRIPT

Phone answered in six rings.

EMPLOYEE: Good afternoon XXXX Ltd.

CALLER: Oh, hello. Can you help me? I'm looking for a quote for contract hire please.

EMPLOYEE: Certainly. Can I just ask which area of the country you are phoning from?

CALLER: From Bristol.

EMPLOYEE: Okay, fine. Is it on behalf of a company?

CALLER: Yes it is.

EMPLOYEE: Could I possibly get our sales executive to call you back because she is on the phone at the moment. She would be very glad to phone you back and discuss what you want.

CALLER: Oh, I've got to go out of the office for a little while. Can I call you back?

EMPLOYEE: Yes, you certainly can. You actually need to speak to a sales executive called (*gives name*). She will be able to furnish you with what you need.

CALLER: Okay then. I'll give you a call later.

EMPLOYEE: Okay then. Lovely.

BOTH: Bye.

Analysis

- It was too long before the call was answered.
- A name or department should have been offered.

73

THE POWER OF THE PHONE

- No reason is given for the questions asked.

- A positive point – the employee went out of his way to reassure the caller that the sales executive would be 'glad of the chance' to speak to the customer, indicating an enthusiasm for dealing with customers that is very refreshing.

- Even if the caller had to leave the office, try and get a telephone number. Otherwise you are in danger of losing the call.

- The employee offered the name of the sales executive so the customer knew who to ask for.

Background

The employee sounded very bright and cheery on the telephone. Improving her technique should develop her natural instinct to promote a professional image considerably.

74

CALL TRANSCRIPT

Phone answered in three rings.

EMPLOYEE: Good afternoon XXXX. How can we help you?

CALLER: Oh, hello. Good afternoon. I'd like a quote for contract hire.

EMPLOYEE: Er, yes. Can I ask the name of the company please?

CALLER: Yes it's . . . (*Gives name.*)

EMPLOYEE: I wonder if you could spell that please? (*Caller spells name.*) Can I ask where you are actually based?

CALLER: Yes, we're in Acton.

EMPLOYEE: Right. And er I wonder can I possibly ask how many company cars you have?

CALLER: We've just got the two.

EMPLOYEE: The two . . . Alright, can I ask your name?

CALLER: Yes, it's . . . (*Gives name.*)

EMPLOYEE: Actually the lady you need to speak to, our Area Sales Manager, her name is (*gives name*). Unfortunately she's not in the building this afternoon. I wonder if I could get your telephone number and ask her to ring you on Monday?

CALLER: Well, I did actually want some figures so I could put them to my boss this afternoon.

EMPLOYEE: I'm afraid they can't because, er, all our area sales managers are out this afternoon.

CALLER: So nobody can help me this afternoon?

EMPLOYEE: I'm afraid they can't, no.

CALLER: Okay. Well I'll have to leave it at that. Thank you.

EMPLOYEE: Alright then.

CALLER: Bye.

EMPLOYEE: Bye.

Analysis

■ If all your sales people are out, arrange for them to be able to contact customers. They are only a phone call away.

■ No attempt was made to prevent the customer slipping away.

■ The employee was hesitant (shy/nervous) about asking for some basic information. ('Can I possibly ask?')

Background

This was a regional office of a multi-national company. No-one in the building could help. The business is about helping customers to keep their cars on the road 24 hours a day.

If they can't answer a sales enquiry on a Friday afternoon, how are they going to support the customer once they have signed him up. Do you think they signed him up?

5

Managing telephone contact in your organisation or department

Telephone sales and marketing activities cover a complex mix of activities.

Outbound calls

Once the decision has been made to telephone customers or prospects pro-actively, the main objective is to supply adequate material in an acceptable form to your team. Records which are woefully out of date, and this is not rare (salesmen are notorious for carrying all the best information about customers in their heads), need to be updated. Some companies have found that success is hampered by the fact that they do not have customers' telephone numbers. You could consider buying in lists or using specialist agencies to supply the numbers.

> **'Previously we didn't telephone non-responders to our direct mail campaigns but with a 20 to 30 per cent uptake we will definitely continue to do so in the future!'**

Outbound calls may be to existing or potential customers, and involve such tasks as research, database building and appointment making. Sales may be completed on the telephone and, ideally, appointment making and selling should be treated as separate functions, since one can cancel out the other as an objective. The questioning techniques and structure of the calls are different. When making an appointment you do not want the conversation to get too involved and lead you to answering so many questions that you talk yourself out of the need for an appointment. 'Thank you, you've given me all the information I need so I don't need to see anyone now.'

A telephone sale is more involved and the customer needs a lot of information to make a decision. Switching from one objective to the other, that is from an appointment to a sale, during the call is difficult to achieve even by experienced telecontact staff.

Inbound calls

'It is very important that every client does have one contact that he can ring because clients don't like to have a lot of different telephone numbers for lots of different people. They would like to know that if they do have a query, even if someone else is dealing with it, that there is someone they can come to and say "Look, I'm not happy about this".

'Basically the phone is crucial when you want immediacy – and we believe our customers want to order immediately the goods which they previously obtained by filling out an order form but which didn't actually tell them whether we had the goods. The phone does that now. Ninety five per cent of our orders come by telephone!'

77

Inbound calls may be prompted by marketing activity such as press advertising or direct mail. Or they could be queries from existing or potential customers who require more information about your service or product. These calls also fall into the category of 'customer service' and could flag up problems or complaints which need to be dealt with in the appropriate manner.

Whilst larger companies may have the resources to maintain telesales, marketing and customer service activities as separate functions within their organisations, this may not be a practical option for most small companies. However, common management principles apply to all, and the following is a guide for any manager who finds himself responsible for managing and motivating any team engaged in telephone activity on behalf of a company.

For anyone who has had the experience of being 'passed around' an organisation, the need to eliminate this practice from your own organisation will need no further explanation. Some of the practical things you can do to make it easier for customers to contact you are:

■ Use your company's telephone number on all printed material, not just correspondence.

- Appoint key people in each department to be responsible for taking messages and passing them on.
- Encourage your staff to take ownership of the call.
- If you have different telephone numbers for different areas of the business, publicise them in a user friendly format, eg a laminated plastic card that customers could carry in a wallet.
- Introduce standards which make your staff aware of the importance of picking up a ringing telephone on three to four rings.
- If staff are unavailable because of meetings, sickness etc, advise everyone who is likely to be covering for them in their absence, of how long they will be away and offer alternative contacts.
- Always fully brief your switchboard about staff absences and changes of responsibility.
- Use ansaphones only if absolutely necessary and check the machine regularly.
- If the volume of incoming calls is great, eg an enquiry centre or order taking department, monitor the flow of traffic. Identify the peaks and staff accordingly. If necessary use part time shift operators to ensure adequate cover.

78

How to integrate outbound and inbound calls

In an ideal world it should be possible to achieve a balance between the two activities, however this is not easy to achieve in practice. Where an organisation receives a high volume of inbound calls there is always the danger of callers being kept waiting for a long period of time because lines are engaged or they are caught up in a queue system. This happens when employees are encouraged to extend the call in an effort to identify selling opportunities or to make outgoing calls to find new customers or to contact existing ones. Whilst this is a desirable objective (many companies would love to receive this sort of volume of calls from customers who want to do business with them, most of their marketing effort goes into stimulating such a response) it does create the danger of alienating your existing customers in your efforts to find new ones.

Equally frustrating for a business is an outbound team caught up with answering incoming enquiries when their prime purpose is to find new business or an inbound team waiting for the telephone to ring! To reconcile the two activities you could consider the following:

- Keep the two functions separate, this allows each team to concentrate on specific tasks. The team handling inbound calls will build up a bank of experience and product knowledge which will enable them to move into a more pro-active sales role with confidence as the opportunity arises. This is most appropriate where the volume of incoming calls is always high.

- Where the calls fall into a consistent pattern, use your telephone management call stats. to help you identify the peaks and troughs; you can then allocate certain parts of the day to experiment with outgoing calls. This will help you to avoid customers having problems getting through to your company and to maximise the productivity of your team.

- Your team may favour receiving a mix of incoming and outgoing calls as it provides them with different telephone situations throughout the day and therefore makes their work more interesting. Do, however, be aware that this may lead to certain members of the team using the number of incoming calls they have taken to avoid making outgoing calls, if they perceive this activity to be less enjoyable.

79

Some companies have chosen the route of directing all incoming calls from potential or existing customers to one central resource. This is fine if you are satisfied that the team can cope, but you do run the risk of overloading them at certain parts of the day. Finally, remember that if you have an outbound team it makes sense to allow them to concentrate on making calls and unless the incoming calls are sales enquiries it is sensible to screen them from any distractions such as general customer queries.

Using a telecontact team tactically

Occasionally companies fail to anticipate an unusually large response to a mailshot and the result is that the telecontact team are forced to react in 'panic' mode. Even in these circumstances the team can still be effective, but to make it truly rewarding it will always benefit you to try and use them in a planned and constructive way. You will enjoy more significant and consistent success if you work out your overall objective and then define your team's role within those parameters.

A common error is for too many departments to get involved in the management of the telecontact team. The team's activities could be the focus of interest from sales, customer service, marketing, PR as well as operational departments. All of these have their own objectives and will approach the team for help in achieving them whilst at the same time not understanding that from the team's point of view the message is unclear as to what the real objectives are. So, for example, different product groups may be running different advertising campaigns in which they would like to involve the telecontact team. There may be a customer care programme under way and of course cold calling must always be considered part of the overall activity. What then happens is that the team is pulled in too many different directions at once thus failing to achieve overall company objectives.

It isn't at all unusual to find several campaigns running at the same time which, whilst aimed at different segments of the market and therefore not causing a clash in marketing, do create a telecontact clash when in one week you may receive several thousand calls and in another week hardly any at all. The best way to use a telecontact team is to include them in your marketing plans right from the very beginning. Look at the campaigns that you are running and the resources you have. Try to plan campaigns so that they flow throughout the year and are unlikely to create peaks of demand which cannot be met. There has been a lot of debate about whether a telecontact team should be used to follow up direct mail activities. I can tell you that I come down firmly on the side of the Telephone-Mail-Telephone school of thought.

First of all, you greatly enhance the prospects of your direct mail activities reaching people who, as well as being potentially interested in what you have to say, are indeed the people who can influence any future decisions an organisation may make when choosing a new supplier. I am talking, of course, about 'decision makers'. A simple telephone call can ensure that you target your mailing effectively. If an organisation is simply not interested in what you have to offer, why bother mailing to them? Strike them off your list and find another prospect who is interested. No matter how good the creative material of a direct mailshot may be, it will not be effective if it doesn't reach the right audience for your message, and worse, it implies that you are inefficient and wasteful.

How a telecontact team can affect your business and your employees

If you are considering introducing a telecontact team into your business you need to consider several issues. Probably the most important is the impact that the team will have on the rest of the business.

A telecontact team is in constant touch either with your customers or with prospective buyers. As information gatherers they are beyond compare. A small team of only six people can each make up to 80 calls a day. They will probably speak to something in the region of 30 effective contacts. Effective contacts being people who are in a position either to make a purchasing decision or at least to influence it. Even this small team of six can speak to 900 potential purchasers each week and leave an impression with a further 1500, so as well as gathering information for you, they are ambassadors for your company. Because of the high profile contact that they have with your customers, a telecontact team is usually the first to be alerted to signs of competitor activity or dissatisfaction among your customers. You need to be able to view responses that they get and then pass on to you with a positive attitude. Remember they are telling you the negative things because they want you to be able to put them right. After all, people do like to talk about their businesses and indeed many products or services have been introduced simply because of the feedback given to telecontact teams by potential customers and existing customers.

81

The team usually demands the same high standards they set for themselves from people elsewhere in the business. For your telecontact team the urge to respond to customer enquiries immediately is overwhelming. They can easily be frustrated if other departments within the business do not operate to their own high standards. It is important that other departments within the business recognise the need to respond quickly to requests for help from the team. Negative comments such as 'I'm too busy' or 'Can I call you back tomorrow' won't help your telecontact team to convey the right sort of impression to your customers.

Remember that when a customer contacts you or has been contacted by you, if the result of that conversation is a problem then you really need to give urgent attention to solving it quickly, and if you are a manager of a telecontact team you must be aware how badly they can be affected by what is seen to be incompetence or indifference from elsewhere in the company. Of course, this may not necessarily be incompetence – they may genuinely be stretched beyond their resources. If this is the case, then you need to talk to managers of those departments concerned to see if there are any ways you can work mutually together to try and speed up those responses.

You should at least be aware that your team may be subject to negative influences. This is the last thing you want because it can be carried over into the telephone conversation with the customer. If your people aren't sure that your company can respond quickly, how on earth can they be expected to persuade customers that it can do so? If their expectations are unrealistic, then you need to take time out with them to sort out what is realistic. Agree procedures between yourselves and other departments and make sure that people stick to them. A helpful way of ensuring a common understanding is to invite managers of other departments along to your team meetings.

Another crucial area where the team may have tremendous impact is on your existing sales force. You need to be aware that a field sales force may view the introduction of telephone contact negatively. Of course, your idea is to supply them with qualified appointments, or to allow them to spend more time developing their territory, but you do need to be aware that they may not always see this as being the case and you must take steps to reassure them about what it is that you intend to achieve with the introduction of the telecontact team. Failure to communicate in this area can lead to the creation of an 'us and them' situation, with the telecontact team feeling that the sales team don't understand their objectives or support them and the field sales team thinking that they may be vulnerable, especially if the telecontact team achieves outstanding successes.

Of course, your field sales team may actually go entirely the opposite way and have huge expectations of what the team can do for them. As a manager you need to make some firm decisions. There is a school of thought that says an appointment is an appointment. As long as it is with a purchasing decision maker, it doesn't really matter whether that company is in the market for your goods or not. The other school says 'I don't want my field sales people talking to anybody unless they are in the frame for making a buying decision now. The truth is probably somewhere between the two. Of course you don't want to waste the valuable resource that your field sales executives represent. It is expensive and time consuming to send them on calls that are going to be non-productive, however, not every appointment is going to result in an order, much as we would like it to be.

Therefore if your telecontact team is making appointments for a field sales team, you need to be very sure in your own mind about what constitutes a good appointment. Draw up the criteria. Make sure they are writing and every member of your team has a copy – and of course every member of the field sales team. This should help to clear up any misunderstandings between the two groups. A sales executive who feels he's been sent on a wild goose chase can feel negative about your company all day. This, of course, is the last thing you want when they're out in the field. However, somebody who goes out and has the opportunity either to do business or sow the seeds for doing business will feel very positive towards the organisation. You also need to remember that views can be subjective so if accusations are flying around, it is important to hear both sides of the story first. This may seem to state the obvious but there is a tendency, because of the heightened tension in telephone selling and telephone marketing, to treat each drama as a crisis. You need to be aware that the other side of the story needs investigating. What may on the face of it appear to be an isolated incident could in fact indicate a pattern of which you are unaware. Constant feedback from telesales executives saying that sales executives have not kept appointments and the constant feedback from field sales that the telecontact team don't make 'qualified' appointments will alert you to problems that need to be sorted out.

83

If each group is given full recognition, and a sufficient amount of time is spent developing the concept, it will reward you well. Planning and consultation is vital.

The advantages and disadvantages of developing a telecontact team

'It's an alternative service for clients, making it as easy as possible for them to do business with us. It provides a friendly touch – the fact that ten to twelve thousand people get in touch with Vernons every week and hear a nice friendly voice and go off the phone with a nice glow and say 'That's a nice company to deal with' and hopefully tell their friends. Our telesales team improves the service we give and helps us to keep our customers.'

ADVANTAGES

The biggest advantage of developing your own team is that they can keep in touch with all of your customer base as well as identifying prospects for you to do business with. The team can allow you to segment your customer base, focusing the activities of your field sales executives where they are most likely to be productive, either in chasing new business or in maintaining existing accounts which are of a complex nature. If you maintain a small external field sales activity, you may find it difficult to support your customer base nationwide. A telephone contact team will help you to do this.

A large sales force is expensive to fund. Every visit costs a significant sum of money (£90 per call is average). Your objective obviously would be to try to make every visit as productive as possible, hopefully resulting in further orders for your company. A telecontact team will support your sales effort by qualifying appointments and identifying prospective business for you. They can telephone every likely prospect within a town and only take a day or two to do it, whereas a field sales executive would take many months to achieve similar results. In this way you can focus the activities of your field sales executives in the most productive way.

Regular telephone contact with your existing customer base means that you will never have a situation where a problem exists and is allowed to fester to the point of a serious catastrophe for relations between you and the customer. Telephone contact can ensure that the account runs smoothly and that your customer remains happy with the level of service or with the goods that you are offering. Any doubts can quickly be resolved and talked through. Often major accounts are retained by companies simply because they are able to pinpoint a particular problem and take swift action to solve it.

One company, for example, maintained telephone contact with an account which was worth half a million pounds to them. As part of its regular 'care call' programme, the telephone executive became aware that changes were taking place in the company which would affect their buying decision in the future. There had been a change of managing director and a manager who had previously been responsible for purchases relating to this service, which was the purchase of company cars, was now being designated to take over other duties. The MD felt that because of this change it was appropriate to invite other potential suppliers in and indeed to look at the whole method of acquisition of the company cars. Because of swift action taken by the telephone sales executive which resulted in field sales visits and a planned programme of communication involving presentations, written material and so forth, the managing director was happy to remain with his existing supplier. But it is absolutely certain that, had any significant period of time lapsed between the new managing director coming into the company and the subsequent meetings that took place, this account would have been in serious danger.

Only by maintaining close links with your customers can you avoid such catastrophes. People in organisations change all the time. Either they move on to a new job or, far more likely, there is restructuring within the company which then moves new people into the frame – people with whom you have to establish relationships. It's very difficult to track these changes purely by making field sales visits simply because of the limited number of visits that can be made each day. However, you can maintain good company intelligence through telephone contact.

Although it is always true to say that your own employees will bring a superior level of commitment, dedication and working knowledge of the company to the job, external agencies can be extremely useful at the point where you are setting up a team and may not have either the necessary management or telephone skills, or knowledge of systems to establish such a team successfully. However, by utilising your employees' knowledge of the business, you will always maintain that extra edge over your competitors.

85

It is important to bear in mind that in today's business environment speed is vital. It is probably for this reason alone that there has been such an incredible boom in personal communication. Every businessman in the country today either has, or is thinking of getting a personal mobile telephone. The need to keep in touch both with the business and with customers is deemed to be vital and a telecontact team is part of this response to the need for an organisation to be available to customers at all times.

The presence of an in-house telecontact team also has the tremendous advantage of allowing you to develop staff into field sales executives in low risk situations. The sheer volume of calls handled will soon provide newcomers to the business with a full grounding in your company's products and services. This allows you to fill field sales appointments immediately and at a very cost effective rate, whilst also reducing the possibility of losing customers during the time a territory is vacant and unattended.

DISADVANTAGES

A major disadvantage, of course, is cost. Switching to telephone customer sales and service will not necessarily save money immediately; investment has to be perceived as a long term commitment to improving the quality of service to a customer which will be returned by maintaining market position. Supporting a telecontact team is not cheap. Systems can be expensive and if you are determined to support your people with computer based data the cost can run into many hundreds of thousands for a team of maybe 70 to 80 people. This can lead to the temptation to use external resources but the more money you spend investing in your own company resources, the more responsive you are going to be in the future. The establishment of a telecontact team has to be seen as an investment. Sometimes companies will make the comment 'we tried it and it didn't work!' Closer investigation, however, almost always reveals that they did not give it a long enough period to become established as a part of the organisation. It is impossible to set up a telecontact team on the basis that if it doesn't start to produce results within three months then the project will be abandoned.

86

Summary

Telephone relationships, just as face to face relationships, need time to build up. A bank of knowledge needs to be built up before they can become truly effective. Your team may ring 1000 prospects and as a result of that end up with 500 or 600 diaried telephone appointments to call those prospects back at a time when they are more likely to be in the market. These are good qualified prospects. From there you could expect a further 50 per cent to result in qualified appointments for your field executives. Of course, the numbers used here are only used as a general example. The point is that will take time to build up relationships and to build up a bank of prospects that you know will be in the market or likely to be in the market when you call.

If the telecontact team is new to your company, they also need to learn about who you are and what you do. Induction courses are very useful as a means of introducing new recruits to the company's philosophy, products and services etc, but it does take time to build up the level of knowledge that is needed to deal with telephone enquiries. The customer on the other end of the phone expects the person who takes the call to have the answers and not to be referred elsewhere. For them to gain that level of knowledge they need to spend some time learning about you and your organisation.

Anybody who has tried telecontact and found that it didn't work almost certainly has not allowed enough time and investment to make it successful. There are many organisations who, although originally scep- tical, have become converts. They started by testing or researching the potential of engaging in telephone marketing, or they used the services of an agency to test the introduction of a new product by phone. What- ever they may have done, they were surprised at the positive response they got and this encouraged them to develop their own in-house resource. There is no doubt that good professional telecontact work is effective. However, it can seem to be a daunting prospect if you are considering introducing it for the first time. The most common reserva- tion is that the product or service may be inappropriate for marketing by telephone. If the service you provide is of a complex or technical nature, you may feel that such issues cannot successfully be explored via the telephone. Or perhaps when you sell your product or service, a contract needs to be signed prior to delivery. All these things can be overcome with good planning and a determined attempt to provide the support necessary for a telecontact team to be effective. For example, you could try making your documentation more streamlined, without infringing on your legal obligations.

87

One company overcame the problem of giving technical advice by opening a helpline staffed by fully qualified post-graduate telecom- munications engineers. Their customers buy communication parts and equipment. The order taking department is extremely busy, taking in the region of between 7000 and 8000 telephone calls each day. Because of the complexity of the goods on offer, the order takers didn't always have the technical ability to answer questions and indeed this was not always desirable as their main objective was to ensure that no customer wanting to place an order was kept waiting longer than 60 seconds from the point of ringing. This helpline ensured that such queries could be speedily rerouted to somebody who was professionally qualified to help them. This extra service provided by the organisation not only did a lot to enhance customer satisfaction but also ensured that when customers did order, they were more likely to order the appropriate parts and make fewer mistakes at a cost both to the company in terms of accepting returned goods and the customer who would risk experiencing further delays before his problem was sorted out.

Resources

THE WORK ENVIRONMENT

The office should be as visually stimulating as possible. Your staff are office bound and, unlike field sales executives, they do not get the opportunity to add variety to their day by visiting different types of businesses. Each operator should have their own work station with sufficient storage space to help them maintain an orderly working area. If your team do not have the advantage of a computer based system you will find that their work space can become very untidy. Leads, mailings and paper prospect lists quickly accumulate and can overflow onto floor space if not filed regularly, preferably within arm's reach of the operator. Telecontact units can soon descend into chaotic abandon if you fail to provide the resources necessary to keep paper in check.

Some managers and operators prefer their space to be surrounded by some sort of screen. This helps to keep distractions to a minimum and allows operators to concentrate on their calls. It is very much a matter of personal taste: some operators feel that screens detract from a team spirit and dislike them because they say it makes them feel as if they are caught in a cage. Although there is no hard and fast rule in this matter, the team as a whole needs to be protected from external noise and intrusion. Other employees should be discouraged from wandering in and out as they will engage in conversations and keep operators off the phone. If you have to share equipment with other departments or staff, such as a photocopier, position it as far away from the team as possible.

Acoustic ceiling tiles help to keep down background noise. A silent department is undesirable – and impossible if telephones are in use – but noise should be of the productive hum variety, not so unbearable as to make it impossible to hear what someone is saying during the call. If your building faces a busy road, try to locate the department to the rear of the building or, if this is not possible, double glaze the windows to keep traffic noise out. Heating and ventilation should be adequate. Ideally staff should have easy access to hot and cold drinks which should be available at all times – talking on the telephone all day is thirsty work!

The need to leave a desk should be kept to a minimum. If your staff are away from their telephones they are unproductive and, worse, unavailable to your customers.

ADMINISTRATION

Wherever possible, have administrators available to support your team. They should be designated telecontact administrators. If you have to share resources from an administrative pool, this can lead to problems when it comes to checking the progress of paperwork. Delays will cause difficulties for your team as it is they who are speaking to your customers.

Do everything you can to streamline your order processing. Telecontact operators who are saddled with unwieldy administration procedures become very unhappy as it prevents them from doing what they are best at – talking to your customers.

TELEPHONE SYSTEMS

These can be as sophisticated as you like – the only constraint is money! One essential item is a headset. Holding a telephone receiver all day is very uncomfortable and restricts the operator's movements. They also find it difficult to take notes. Some employees may be resistant to the introduction of headsets but you can reassure them that after using them for a week they will wonder how they ever managed without them.

Any complaints you may receive from staff about difficulties in hearing what people are saying to them on the phone should always be taken seriously and investigated immediately. If the telephone is not functioning properly, it severely limits your operators' effectiveness when they are using the telephone.

The choice of telephone systems now available is enormous and therefore can be very confusing. Mistakes can be costly and it is both practical and necessary to seek advice from objective sources. Ask suppliers to provide you with the names of companies who have purchased from them and talk to them about the system. Try to establish whether their business needs are similar to your own. ACD (Automatic Call Distribution) systems are only appropriate if you envisage taking a high volume of incoming calls. Call management systems do provide useful information when you are trying to establish whether you have sufficient operators or if they are making enough calls. Equipment is now so sophisticated that a supervision console can tell a manager who is on the phone, what telephone number has been rung and how long the call has lasted. A supervisor can override an operator and in effect 'force' them to accept calls even if they have not put their extension into 'available' mode. In addition, a supervisor can record calls or silently intrude. However, before investing in such equipment, please refer to the legal issues in Chapter 1 concerning their use.

Hints on recruiting the right candidate

'I think the people I've seen who can use the phone are people who first of all generally have a much higher level of concentration. The best telesales person I've been involved with, a lady called Sarah, working only mornings, achieved 50 per cent more than the top sales person working full time. She did it by concentrating with such an intensity that nothing happened in the office of which she had any recollection at all during the four hours she worked. The degree to which she could analyse a customer from a ten minute phone call was awesome. In that time she had established a rapport, estaL lished information and had created her stature as a sales person, and had the customer eating out of her hand. There are lots of examples of people like this.'

First of all, scan your local newspapers and look at the job advertisements for telesales operators. Here we can see people's preconceptions and prejudices come to the fore. Key words are 'self-motivated', surely that must be self-evident, and 'aggressive'. Really? Aggressive is probably the least likely quality that you will want to be looking for. Aggression on the telephone leads to only one conclusion and that is the sound of a telephone being disconnected.

Whilst good presentation skills are a prerequisite, even more important is the ability to listen. Because of this you need to concentrate on identifying listening skills when trying to select the right candidate. When scanning these advertisements you will see that the applicants are invited to write in. I can think of no greater waste of time either for the applicant or the recruiter. Their written skills are subsidiary to their verbal skills and to avoid wasting time in selecting and interviewing candidates, why not eliminate those who are completely unsuitable right at the very start of the process. Ask candidates to call either you or designated colleagues. Be prepared with a list of questions that you wish to ask. For example, you could ask them to explain why they think they have the qualities it takes to be a good telephone contact operator. As in any interview, their answers can be very revealing.

Until the use of videophones becomes accepted practice issues such as age and appearance become almost irrelevant. Naturally you will expect your candidates to conform to the required company standards on dress and so forth, but here you really need to put your preconceptions to one side and consider what the candidate actually sounds like. Are they warm and welcoming? Do they sound cheerful? Do they sound as if they are glad to be talking to you? Do they ask pertinent questions? Do they listen to what you are saying. All of these are far more important factors than appearance: warmth, understanding, patience and tolerance are all vital qualities.

One of the most successful telemarketing operators I ever had whose role was to clean lists of potential contacts for the telephone sales team was well into her 60s and worked very successfully from home. She saw each call as a challenge and was extremely enthusiastic. She thoroughly enjoyed the job and every day would have several stories to tell about her 'derring-do' when ringing up, for example, the chairman of a company. Somehow, whether it was her age or personality, these people would be happy to speak to her because they found it a refreshing change from the quality of call they normally received from other less well-motivated and enthusiastic people.

91

However, generally speaking, youth seems to dominate in the tele-contact team. Whilst this can certainly help generate a lively and stimulating atmosphere, don't forget that experience can be just as important and, indeed, when talking to business people, it may be that you really do need the authoritative voice of an older person.

Sex can be important, too. For example, in the contract hire industry 99.9 per cent of the decision makers are men. They are talking about cars, perhaps their favourite subject, and it is always helpful to have people who are as enthusiastic about cars as the customer is. This generally tends to mean that the operators are male and it would be true to say that in this environment the men can be more successful at getting through to the right contact.

This is by no means common or usual in other areas of business and it is certainly true to say that over the last 20 years the make up of a telecontact team is dominated by women. This is probably because they bring certain skills to the role that women tend to have in abundance. You can have men being just as successful but they need to consider the approach they make to their customers, for example, you wouldn't necessarily want a man ringing a housewife at home. Unless they were very quick to explain the purpose of their call they could create entirely the wrong impression when they first ring.

Good verbal communication skills are essential to success and this is usually a natural result of a good education. Certainly some of the most successful people who have been engaged in a telecontact team have been graduates. Whilst this is by no means necessary, indeed people tend to come from all sorts of backgrounds and bring their different experiences to the team, it is worthwhile ensuring that they do have a sufficient level of education to allow them to choose the kind of words that are appropriate to any given situation and that they are as comfortable talking to a housewife at home as they would be to a chairman of a large organisation.

Telecontact operators, if they don't have the right skills or haven't received the right training, can be very inhibited about making calls to a wide variety of people, and what you don't want, as an employer, is to find that people put off making calls to certain people, especially if they are the prime objective of your team. Shy people may be less comfortable with cold calling. However, their very shyness may make them more empathetic to customers' problems and they could in fact be extremely effective in this role. You need to match their skills with your requirements and vice versa.

To give you an example of the sort of different experience that people may bring to the team, in the past I have successfully recruited a biology graduate, an ex-actress, a self-employed insurance adviser, a waitress, a store assistant who sold up-market china ware, a psychology graduate, and a former sole proprietor of a dress shop. This illustrates my point that there is no one specific background from which you can recruit and be assured that you will recruit successfully. What all of these people had in common was the fact that they were good communicators, they had terrific, though not overwhelming, personalities and they also possessed the ability to listen.

It isn't always necessary to recruit people with previous experience. Whilst this can be helpful if you are setting up a new unit and don't wish to start entirely from scratch, it is a mistake to assume that they will have had the necessary and appropriate training you think they have had. If at all possible, you need to analyse what level of skills they possess. Ask them to talk about their most recent successes. Ask them about their strengths and weaknesses in terms of maintaining good relationships with customers. If they talk enthusiastically of favourite customers, you can be fairly sure that they are dedicated and committed to their job. Indeed, commitment is one of the best characteristics often displayed by any member of a telecontact team. They tend to care very deeply about their customers and about the company for which they work. This caring can sometimes be expressed in a way that may seem hypercritical of either you as a manager or the organisation as a whole, but should not be misunderstood. We are talking about people who desperately want to get it right. They also want you to get it right and are prepared to put their neck on the line to achieve that, even at the risk of incurring wrath. They may often be perceived as forthcoming and direct but remember they are used to using the telephone as a means of communication and we have already mentioned the time restrictions this can place on people. Therefore to move the conversation forward these are the two precise qualifications which will enable them to achieve this. Put it in that context and you may actually be looking at people who have a very useful contribution to make to your business.

THE TELEPHONE INTERVIEW

Use the telephone interview to screen for certain key skills. Use a structured questionnaire to check the following elements.

1. Do they conform to the personal profile you have decided is appropriate for this work?

2. Is their telephone manner satisfactory? Does it convey the image that you wish to convey to your customers?

3. Do they display an ability to handle objections?

4. Are they persuasive?

5. Can they project their personality via the telephone? What sort of mental image have you created from this call?

If your candidate fulfils the criteria, you can then ask them to submit a written application which you can then screen further. This can then be followed by the first interview. It is a good idea also to use the formal interview process to check various other aspects of your candidate. Are they numerate? Do they have good written communication skills to support their verbal communication skills? This is very important if you require them to input information into a database for example. Many databases have been ruined or rendered worthless by the candidate's complete inability to spell. Indeed, one company who takes something in the region of one million telephone calls a week has found it cost-effective to use a system where the address is automatically keyed in on acceptance of a postcode number simply because they have found this to be an enormous problem. If written skills are essential to the process, for example they may be asked to write a letter to customers as a result of the call, you must take care to check this.

It's also a good idea to include as part of the recruitment process an opportunity for the candidate to visit the telecontact team. This will give you the opportunity to see if they fit in well with the rest of the team and also to see how the team reacts to them. Remember that a telecontact team is a very close-knit unit. They work under exceptional circumstances – they are together all day, every day. The team does not need to be made up of like-minded people to be successful. Indeed, this is one area where variety is the spice of life. Nevertheless, you do need to check that the dynamics are right. The choice of the right candidate for telecontact work is, more than any other area, largely instinctive. Basically you have to make a subjective choice since you are recruiting in an area where only some specific skills can be checked and tested thoroughly. For example, if you were recruiting an engineer, an engineering degree followed by documented experience would help you to make a decision, but what we're talking about here is whether this person can communicate with your customers effectively and this is probably one of the hardest areas to judge. You don't have the advantage of being party to their telephone calls.

My best advice would be to go with your instincts. If you like them the chances are that your customers will too. If you have any doubts about them, no matter how urgent the need to fill the vacancy, try to avoid the temptation to 'panic recruit'. This can lead to long term problems. Not only might you offend your customers but you might spoil the balance of your team as well.

How to create a motivating atmosphere

'If you are a good manager you can tell when there is a problem. You can see it either in the way someone is doing their calls, or by what they are saying. It's down to the manager to come in and say "Have you got a problem? What is it? Do you need any help? Is it something I've said?" '

'Yes, incentives do motivate, even little ones like a Mars bar. Everyone comes in and you are doing a 9 to 5 job and damned hard work. If your boss comes in and says "whoever does three sales by 3 o'clock can go home", I think that's really nice when that happens.'

'You have to make it as much fun as possible. Spot motivations

could be: if the job was done you could go home early, or a bottle of
champagne for the person who makes the most appointments in a
month. You need to adapt your style as a manager to the environ-
ment. When you are managing a team and there is a repetitive and
boring element I think it is important that the manager has the
personality to be able to do that. They need to be able to laugh at
themselves because when you have a group of people working
together like that they are going to gang up on you. You have to
have a thick skin and be able to go with the flow and bounce back.'

This is a central requirement to the development of any successful team. Motivation here is probably more important than anywhere else in the business. This is a very tough job. Your team are on the line all day, every day, talking to customers and trying to convey an 'up' image. They have to be 'in the mood' whether you are or not and if your team isn't you will have to find ways to redress this. If you talk to anybody who has experience in managing telephone sales or telephone marketing departments, you will find one of the major issues which tasks them is how to maintain a motivating atmosphere. They are constantly looking for new ways and new ideas to help achieve this.

95

Sometimes the old and tried ideas can be very successful and indeed they should never be excluded from your thinking. However, the more imaginative and creative you can be, the better will be the result. If you find this difficult, ask your team what they would like to do. You will be delightfully surprised by some of the imaginative ideas that they have. The whole point of creating a motivating environment is not only to achieve a lively and productive atmosphere for your team but also to achieve the objectives you may have as their manager. Therefore you can focus your motivational activities on specific areas of the business. For example if you find that your team is not on the telephone as often as you would like them to be you can devise a motivational scheme which will help you improve their productivity.

KEY TECHNIQUES FOR MOTIVATION

It is important that your team understands what you want them to do. You must have very clear objectives and these must be communicated satisfactorily to your team. A good way of ensuring that this is happening is to have regular team meetings at which such subjects may be discussed. Team meetings can be extremely motivational and in a tele-contact environment should never be further apart than once a month. Even better is to have a meeting each week. This could either be at 9.00

am on a Monday morning to set out the objectives for the week or it could be a 'round robin' meeting late on Friday afternoon to summarise the achievements of the week. Some managers favour meetings every day but this may not always be practical. Certainly for the weekly meetings they need be no longer than 30 minutes to an hour but your monthly meetings should be far more structured and these will be discussed in detail further on.

Your team should have the opportunity for a monthly review with yourself at which their performance and standards can be discussed. This is a good opportunity to praise where praise is appropriate and to criticise where criticism is due. Obviously such criticism should be constructive and should conclude with you setting out clear objectives of what you want from next month's performance. Use training plans to motivate and manage the team. The training plan should lead your employee towards filling the training gap that may exist which is preventing them from being successful.

Your department's results should be displayed everywhere and be clearly seen by anybody who visits the department. Telecontact people like to see their achievements recognised and commented on by people within the business. If your department has visitors, and very few visitors can resist the opportunity to visit a telecontact team, usually because it's the liveliest area in the business, then it should be made easy for your visitors to see just what it is that your team is doing.

You should also have NOBO wallboards wherever possible and they should be highlighting the key achievements of your team. It could be the biggest order, it could be highest number of calls that day. It can also be fun – it might contain a quote of something silly that has been said, either by the telecontact operator or a customer. Wherever possible try to use league tables. Telecontact people are very competitive and you need to spur them on to even greater performance levels. So, for example, if you want them to increase the number of calls per day, publish your team's call rate on the board. Get the telecontact team to fill this board in themselves because this helps to create peer pressure. They are often unwilling to put up a low number of calls simply because they will be ribbed by their team mates. As a manager you should capitalise on this.

Incentives of every kind are deemed to be necessary to manage a telecontact team successfully but these incentives do not have to be monetary to be successful and if you are on a limited budget then you really can achieve quite startling results by using methods that cost virtually nothing to run. A manager demonstrated this very clearly by an incredibly successful scheme that he devised and ran effectively for many years. He bought certificates which are freely available in any good stationery shops, which looked very impressive. They weren't quite hand illuminated but they certainly did look quite stunning and they weren't terribly expensive to buy. He set out key objectives for his team – for example they had to hit their targets and they had to do it profitably. He then developed a league table and whoever came top each month was presented with a certificate at the team meeting. The first certificate to be presented to an individual was signed by the manager himself. But should an individual win further certificates, then obviously continuing to receive certificates signed by their sales manager would not have the same motivating effect so he resolved this very simply by setting out a timetable. If they received one certificate it was signed by the sales manager. The second certificate would be signed by the sales director. The third certificate was signed by the operations director. Eventually he worked through the board until after a period of six months, it could be signed by the managing director. Ultimately he went to the chairman of the group who was not only pleasantly surprised to receive the request, but had no problem at all signing the certificate. It cost him nothing, only a moment of his time.

97

When one individual passed the seven certificate step, the pride with which those certificates were displayed on the wall space behind her desk had to be seen to be believed. I don't know quite what happened when the eight certificate was won but, knowing the manager concerned, I'm sure he would have come up with something equally creative. The point is that recognition in itself can be very motivating and certainly this particular scheme had the advantage of motivating individuals in the team to build up a collection. That individual concerned was really motivated by going to the 'n'th degree to win all of the certificates available. The fact that she did so was a tribute not only to her own self-motivation but also to clever prompting by her manager.

Visits to the department can also be made to work for you. If a team is proud of its success and commitment, they really do welcome the opportunity to speak to visitors and to allow themselves the chance to persuade them in person of how effective their work can be. Talk to your managing director, fellow directors or fellow managers. Ask them if they are likely to have any visitors coming in over the next few months who would be interested in visiting the department and speaking directly to the people who work there. For example, if one of your team has made a contact which has led to the successful completion of an order, when the customer comes in to sign that order he may be very happy to meet the first person who spoke to him in your organisation. It will also give your operator the chance to thank the customer for placing his business with them. The reaction from customers who visit this department is that they feel cared for. They are certainly made to feel welcome and it provides a welcome intrusion into the team's day. If managed correctly, it can not only be motivational for your team, but inspirational for your customer.

All of the examples I am going to list below have been culled from successful managers of telecontact operations. They are intended to give you inspiration and spur you on to make greater efforts to create more motivational schemes of your own.

You can devise schemes around the time of year. In the days leading up to Christmas you could have an Advent calendar. Each box could be opened by a telecontact operator on achievement of criteria such as hitting the required number of calls for the day. Or the required number of orders, or whatever your objective is for that day. Include fun ones, like the tidiest desk, the loveliest personality and quality achievements such as the neatest writing on an order. Inside the calendar could be a further question and, if they answer that correctly, they could be awarded a spot prize.

Spot prizes are incredibly effective in this type of atmosphere. Again they don't have to be expensive – I've seen people jealous of somebody who won a £1.25 eyeshadow compact or somebody who won a magician's trick that cost 50 pence! Remember, it's the winning that's important.

Things can be devised around Halloween. That immediately conjures up pictures of witches (a manager is a prime candidate, incidentally, for the witch's costume!). You can bring in decorative features such as devil's forks, pumpkins, skeletons and whatever else you can find that fits the theme. You can have a bonfire theme with fireworks and rockets displayed. Easter Bunnies – for that perhaps your spot prizes could be small Easter eggs leading up to the award of a very large Easter egg to be taken home at Easter. This is incredibly motivating for people with girlfriends or boyfriends that they would like to give the egg to. Doting mums want to give it to their children. You will be surprised at the kind of people who go all out to win this kind of prize.

Theme days can also be centred around nationalities. You could have a Greek day or a French day or an Italian day. For the French day everybody would be required to wear a beret. Perhaps the prizes could be centred around all things French – paté, wine, cheeses and so forth.

A very successful scheme was run by one manager who devised the idea of cutting out from women's magazines extremely tempting pictures of goodies for Christmas – the Christmas turkey, the Christmas pudding, wine, mince pies, sherry and so forth. These were pasted onto card and cut out to make fairly stiff cardboard representations of the sort of things that would go into an average Christmas hamper. In the weeks that ran up to Christmas, as her team achieved certain targets they were awarded a picture of something that would go into a hamper. They each had a sort of 'washing line' arrangement above their desk and the picture of the turkey was pinned on, followed by the Christmas pudding etc. until finally on Christmas Eve they added up who had the most goodies in their hamper. The person who won was promptly awarded a magnificent hamper which had been put together by the manager. Depending on your company's budget, you can make this hamper as big or as small as you like. If you really want to impress, why not consider a hamper delivered by one of this country's top stores?

99

Your schemes can be centred around quizzes, games of trivial pursuit or a treasure hunt. You can increase your team's product knowledge by making the quizzes relevant to the company and organisation in which you work. You might ask them how many customers you have, or what is your most successful product line. These are extremely effective ways of building up product knowledge and can generate just as much intense competition. However, it would be a mistake to use product knowledge exclusively. Throw in some fun questions as well. You can further introduce competition by asking trivial pursuit questions which may be themed or not. If you were having a theme day you might include a quiz in which people would be asked questions about the country concerned.

Bran tubs can be very exciting. Some managers may think this is rather old fashioned and that people aren't turned on by things like bran tubs any more. All I can say is 'Just try it!' A team manager used this idea to keep her team motivated during a slack period in the year. The bran tub itself was quite expensively decorated in a gold and silver theme. It was filled with polystyrene chippings, the sort that provide protective wrapping for computers, and each present had been chosen by all members of the team who had simply been given a budget and asked to select a suitable gift. This involved them at the very start of the competition. Then the presents were wrapped, not necessarily following their original shape, so that there were some very strange looking parcels in the bran tub. People were actually feeling the parcels and trying to guess what was in them. Curiosity was very high. When a winner was chosen at the end of the week, a great show was made of giving them the opportunity to dip in the bran tub. People were just as curious to see what was in the gift as they were about winning it. Indeed, the manager concerned received a complaint from another department who felt they had missed out on this treat and they wanted a bran tub, too! In fact there is no reason at all why managers cannot use this in other areas of the business where people are working closely together, perhaps in administration departments. It's amazing what it can do for morale.

Finally, an idea that has recently come to my attention was to issue 'Task Envelopes'. The envelopes are awarded on achievement of a number of points. Inside is a request to ring somebody nominated in the company. This person will, of course, have been fully briefed by the manager concerned. The idea is to help them develop their questioning skills. By asking the manager concerned the right questions, they should elicit sufficient information to give them a clue to their next envelope. It's almost a kind of treasure hunt but it does rely on their ability to question people over the telephone to achieve certain objectives. It's illuminating not only for the person making the call, but for the manager receiving it, too. Successful completion of the tasks leads to the treasure. Again, the prize need not necessarily be a huge one – for the team, most of the fun is in the winning.

It is important to recognise that, sitting at a desk all day, perhaps doing very structured, repetitive calls, can be extremely tiring and boring. If your employees were making widgets, this would still be a problem, though one that could be contained internally. However, these particular employees are representing your company and you want them to convey the best image possible. The more time you spend devising motivational games and competitions, the greater the return from your team will be. This is not pandering to childish instincts – indeed, tele-contact teams are usually noted for their diligence and job commitment. However, they do thrive on recognition and if you don't seem to care, they won't care, and then your customer will think, quite rightly, that **you don't care!**

How to measure results

'Our standards cover all aspects of telephone communication. Ninety-five per cent of calls must be answered in 15 seconds, which we think is the appropriate number of rings.

'Every member of staff is checked for quality each week. Was the style of answering in the style that the client had asked for? Was the content correct? Did they give a welcome to the customer? Did they say thank you very much? Did they control the call well or did they just let the customer ramble on? Did both parties get a mutually acceptable resolution at the end of the call? All this gets fed back to the staff member.'

First of all you have to measure activity. This can be best achieved by using a combination of call management systems and a tick sheet. Whilst call management systems are useful, they only allow you to measure the number of telephone calls that are either made or received within a given time. If you are running a large telephone contact team it can certainly help you to identify areas where you may not be covered by sufficient staff at certain times. For example, tea breaks, lunch breaks or there may be an upsurge in telephone activity during certain hours, depending on the kind of business you are in. These systems will help you analyse the volume of calls that flow in and out of your organisation, and help you to ensure that telephone calls do not go unanswered. They will also tell you how long your operators are actually speaking on the telephone. You may be surprised to find that full time operators may spend, out of an eight hour working day, as little as three to three and a half hours actually speaking on the phone. This can be an indication of one of two things: either your administration processes are so complex that they are not able to spend as much time as they would like on the telephone, or the flow of work is not correctly managed. A realistic expectation of how long people should actually spend speaking on a telephone is about four to four and a half hours a day, although if they are totally supported by a computer system which enables them to key in information during the call, thus freeing them from any administration, it could be as much as five to six hours.

Having assessed the volume of telephone calls, you need to look at the type of calls. If your team is essentially a proactive one making calls out of the business, you need also to monitor carefully the type of calls they are handling. A telephone contact team, by their very nature, are com-

102

TICK SHEET ANALYSIS

Operator: Date: Project:

NAME RUNG	EFFECTIVE CONTACTS	RESULT

*The tick sheet can be as complex or as simple as you like. You can add keys to gather more information in the results box eg alpha keys: A = 1 order B = 2 orders or A = highly satisfied B = highly dissatisfied municative and customer orientated. Therefore they can become the obvious choice for anyone in your organisation to route a call through. If they are being tied up in sorting out customer problems when you need them to be on the telephone either selling or account managing, or whatever their prime function is, then you have a problem. This could be the result of an organisation where inbound calls are passed to your team unnecessarily. It may be that you need to reassess how calls are routed in your business. It could identify a need for a customer enquiry desk, or it could simply be a matter of retraining your switchboard operators to enable them to route calls more successfully to the approp-riate departments.

Sophisticated database management systems will allow you to gather information about how frequently your customers are being called and of course the placing of an order will enable you to measure success directly. Because of the fast rate of change in business in the last few years, all too often database systems are 'stand alone' – that is they don't necessarily integrate to other computer systems which may be used in your organisation. Therefore the opportunity to directly correlate the volume of calls with results isn't always easily available unless you are fortunate enough to have had a custom built computer system.

There are some simple ways that you can achieve similar results. Unfortunately they are paper driven but they will give you so much more in the way of management information that, in the absence of an integrated database and telephone system, the time invested in main-taining these paper driven systems will certainly be well spent. A tick sheet will help you to gather any information you need. As the name implies, information is recorded by means of ticking appropriate boxes. 'Ticks' reduce the amount of writing your team has to do. A simple version of a tick sheet is shown in Fig. 5.1.

The sheet illustrated allows you to record the number of companies rung, whether an effective contact was achieved, and the result, which may be an order, a diary call back or whatever. You can use these sheets to gather more complex information but try to collect only information that you will use. Sometimes it is tempting to try and gather lots of information which ultimately ends up lying in somebody's drawer.

Using alphabetic keys can enable you to gather a reasonable volume of information in a simple way. In the example shown I have used A = 1 order or B = 2 orders and so forth, or you could use it to indicate the satisfaction level of customers. If your team is using material that comes from different sources, for example they may be following up direct mail campaigns, you could use a key to indicate which campaign they are currently working on. You can further divide the tick sheet to enable you to record the number of outgoing calls and incoming calls if you have no call management system. This is a fairly crude way to record activity. However, my experience is that people are generally very honest about the level of activity they engage in and the tick sheets can give you meaningful management information.

Use the tick sheets to average out the volume of activity and the results your team is achieving. Use the average to establish a benchmark. Below average results, of course, would indicate a need for some action by yourself.

Below is a list of the kind of activity you can record:

- The number of companies rung.
- Whether the call was inbound or outbound.

- The number of effective contacts, that is to say people your team has spoken to who have the ability to make, or at least influence, a decision.
- The result of the call: that is if an appointment follows, a sale or some action is required by your department.
- The source of the call: for example enquiries received from direct mail activity, advertising, public relations and so forth.
- The type of call – that is it could be a cold call, account management, a follow up call to a previous conversation, or a care call.

Even if the telephone contact in your department is not of a sales nature, you can still use the tick sheet to measure telephone activity. It would be helpful for you to know how many incoming calls come into the department and what happens as a result of those calls – that is to say what sort of activity is generated as a result of the conversation. The tick sheet will enable you to build up a picture of the effectiveness of handling telephone calls within your department and will give you management information to enable you to take the necessary steps to see that calls can be dealt with in a satisfactory way.

The decision to buy a case of wine will probably not take as long as the decision to buy capital equipment and therefore each service or industry will produce its own standards. As a broad rule of thumb, if you are 'cold calling' you can expect effective contacts to be approximately 40 per cent of the number of companies rung and from this you would expect to generate sales from about five per cent of the effective contacts you have made, although I do stress that this will vary from company to company. By summarising the results gained from the tick sheet you should be able to establish a satisfactory norm for your own business and use this as the standard required from the team.

It is also a good idea to ring your organisation or the people within your own department from time to time. If your staff recognise you, then nominate a fellow manager to do this. Check that the standards you have introduced are being followed. The sort of things that you could check up on are the amount of time it takes for the phone to be answered: whether a corporate response was offered and whether the person who took the call offered their own name. You can also look at things like knowledge of your product, company or service – whether the person who took the call was helpful – did they know enough about your organisation to be able to help you? Once you have decided what sort of things you want to measure, you can devise a standard form to enable you to do this and award score points for each part of the telephone call. The call analysis sheet will help you to identify some key areas. You can then publish these results on a monthly basis. This will help to establish that people are aware of the standards you expect from telephone calls and it should be a source of pride if a department scores 100 per cent.

105

Summary

Many companies are naturally reluctant to invest in sophisticated telephone and business computer database systems without some idea of the return. Each company is different, and a manager will have to conduct substantial research into how customer communications work in his own company.

The technology is improving all the time, and its application has to be carefully considered, eg automatic voice response systems may be appropriate for communicating simple messages, but are completely unable to cope with complex transactions.

Current sales statistics have to be analysed and the cost of a sale carefully measured. Some aspects can be dealt with more efficiently via the telephone, such as account management, whilst the signing of contracts may still need to be done face to face. However, some very simple measuring techniques will help you to get started.

Certainly, companies who have used a telecontact team to improve their direct mail responses have succeeded in doing so, and account management activities can dramatically improve renewal and add-on business. Frequent customer contact is not always achievable in the field and can, with proper use of the telephone, create a lot of opportunities for up selling and cross selling.

6

When do you telephone?

A look at current practice in business

The use of written communication in business and the professions

'I'd rather ring than send a memo because you get so many memos about different things you tend to pile them up until you've got nothing else to do and then go through them, whereas if you pick up the telephone it's so much easier.'

'Quite often I receive memos which may just be one line to confirm a meeting, when it has already been confirmed verbally. Some people send a fax followed by a letter and then a phone call. As long as they have everything written down they're happy.'

'I would say that if, prior to my arrival there were 100 memos a week, there are now two. Memos cost money but more importantly they don't communicate. I can send you a memo and you may or may not respond. I can ring you and I can say what I want and this is why. You can't do that in a memo. The phone call is more personal, more considered. I like to talk to the staff. I chat to people and they communicate. For each company letter I speak to each member of staff half a dozen times.'

It is still common practice in the professions to write to a customer, client or patient, asking them to ring to arrange an appointment. Or, worse, arbitrarily selecting a time without prior consultation, thus generating delays, further discussion, or worst of all, 'no-shows' which create unproductive gaps in the work schedule.

Direct contact by telephone to confirm an appointment gains commitment to the time and cuts out unnecessary delays when trying to organise a schedule. It may be difficult to contact customers, patients or clients during normal working hours but it is still worthwhile discovering whether they can be contacted. Your customer may work different hours from yourself, he may be able to accept calls at his workplace or there could be a partner at home who could take messages. The assumption that it is not possible to ring may be disproved if you ask him how he prefers to be contacted. If a written communication is necessary, always supply a direct line telephone number and contact name to allow the caller the opportunity to cancel or rearrange with the minimum of effort.

Paperwork and its administration is expensive. Whilst computer technology has done much to reduce the mountains of files, memos and correspondence lying in dusty boxes, it is by no means without faults. Computer generated correspondence is generally of a fairly uniform nature. Although it can be personalised, because the body copy is standard it never quite manages the informal, friendly tone the sender would like. Unfortunately, it can also be inaccurate, particularly if it is automatically generated and the subject of the correspondence is already under discussion. A customer may be querying a bill and be sent a standard reminder letter even though he has been allowed extra time until the query is resolved. Even when companies go to great lengths to customise letters and pay more attention to their choice of words, it is by no means certain that the customer will understand the message.

Internal memos can cause a lot of resentment because the tone may be perceived to be carping or critical when the writer merely meant to be succinct. They also depersonalise the message and can create unnecessary ill feeling or resentment. Some managers may feel that memos are useful because they confirm what is required and so avoid misunderstandings. However, you do need to be aware that some recipients simply feel they are sent to cover a manager's back. If you are changing accepted practice or introducing new ideas or concepts, these are nearly always more effectively communicated, at least initially, verbally because they allow room for flexibility and changes to your original idea which may result from the conversations you have.

Memos also slow down the business process because the people who receive them tend to stockpile them with the intention of reading them when they have time. Thus urgent changes may not be implemented when the sender would wish. 'Urgent' memos that require immediate action are doomed from the start! **If it's that urgent, telephone!**

A memo asking for a reply to a previous memo is a waste of paper! If the purpose is to elicit a response and not simply to score points – **pick up the telephone!** Sending out reminder letters is also a duplication of effort. If a reply has not been received to the first one, a second is likely to have only a minimal effect. You can use the telephone to prompt people to pay bills or renew subscriptions and improve the flow of cash into your company.

If the people you wish to contact are unavailable, you may be tempted to send out a memo as at least you can say they have been advised. You might like to consider the use of telephone systems which allow you to make one phone call and contact all recipients, as their telephone numbers are pre-programmed and the message is logged at a certain checking point which your staff or colleagues can call each day. This avoids tying up your secretarial resources. It is much quicker and achieves the same end.

Fortunately, the trend is towards trusting that a request for action, when made by telephone, is increasingly more likely to be acted upon. As people grow more used to communicating by telephone they will treat such requests more attentively than in the past. Not all written communication is replaceable by using the telephone but the amount can be reduced substantially and this will have the added benefit of allowing more time for your secretary to carry out less mundane tasks than taking shorthand or filing memos.

If staff are trained to gather information via the telephone, it can establish the true situation more effectively than via a written communication. A telephone conversation is more intimate, and therefore a customer or colleague may be more forthcoming than when expressing himself in writing. Written responses are more likely to be couched in formal terms and true feelings may be difficult to gauge. A telephone call allows you to draw conclusions that a written response never would. The tone of voice: hesitation, friendliness or evasiveness, all provide clues for you to use.

How to enhance written communication and make it easier for your customer or client to contact you

'I've noticed that people are increasingly using the telephone to solve their problems rather than writing. We now have a direct dialling system and if people know they can get directly through to you without being diverted or put on hold they will get in touch with you.'

Direct mail which relies on prospects responding via a coupon loses opportunities where a customer may prefer to respond by telephone. Obviously, most customers are busy people and the telephone is a very quick way of indicating interest. It may be that this interest relates to the desire to gain more information and what could be easier than to fill in the gaps in your knowledge by responding by telephone because then you and the company who has written to you can both work together to identify whether a need really exists for a product or service.

Surprisingly, direct mail tends to be the baby of the marketing department. The sales department is in many ways considered to be marketing's customers and yet time after time mailings leave the marketing department with no means of identifying that quick route of communication for the customer. Where a telephone number is included it is often an afterthought. It isn't displayed prominently and not enough consideration is given to the sort of number that might be used, whether it should be, for example, a freephone number or a number that would be charged at local rates for the caller, or whether the telephone number is easy to remember. The choice of a telephone number may be one which doesn't always direct the customer to a resource that can handle the call.

Direct mail is a very effective way of communicating. It allows you to explain complex subjects in detail without overloading the customer with too much information in a conversation. It can substantiate what your sales people have already said or indeed provoke fresh avenues of interest among your customers. However, it should be reinforced with a telephone call.

More and more organisations today are looking at integrating their direct mail activities with a telephone follow up. This is necessarily a fairly costly thing to do and as such isn't available to everybody in business. But there is something you can do to establish that telephone contact and that is to make it easy for the customer to identify which number to ring for more information. If you decide to do this it is important to brief the people who may be involved in handling these incoming enquiries. It's no good at all, having given your customers a chance to ring, if the people answering the calls are not adequately prepared for the kind of questions they are likely to receive. If your direct mail involves a coupon facility for customers, by all means use this, but don't put your telephone number on the coupon! This is because someone may clip out a coupon intending to return it but retain the rest of your material for future reference. Should they need to contact you at some time in the future they would find it difficult to do so simply because the telephone number is no longer there. The coupon is in a drawer, forgotten, the intention to send it not followed through with action!

If it is appropriate to your promotion you can also use the phone number in a flash across the envelope but of course this will only work with certain products or services on offer. For example Vernons Pools use a freephone telephone number splashed across the envelope which contains the coupon, giving their customers the opportunity to renew their business directly with their telesales team. However, an accountant may feel a little inhibited about such a practice. Your telephone number can also be included on business cards, advertising material, address stickers or anything on which your address would normally appear. Wherever possible, make it easier for your customers to contact you by phone rather than in writing.

If you are writing a letter to a client or a customer that requires a response from them, it may be more convenient to them to respond by telephone rather than in writing. Therefore you should make it easy for them to do so. Give a telephone number on which you are available and if possible make it your direct line, so that they do not experience any unnecessary delays in coming through to you. If you are a manager who is away from the business a lot, why not include your car phone number as well?

If you know there are times when you will be unavailable, it is helpful to indicate this in your letter. For example, you may attend a regular weekly sales or management meeting which is not usually interruptable. Indicate that there are times when you may not be available and offer an alternative number for customers to ring should they wish to do so.

Maximising PR activity

If your company is featured in trade or professional magazines, newspapers, television or radio, this will prompt reaction from customers or prospects. It is embarrassing if their first contact with your organisation results in a blank response from your employees. Make the most of your publicity by circulating to all employees a copy of the piece and indicating how you would like them to respond. Brief them as fully as possible and consider what the content of such enquiries may be. This is even more important if the publicity is about some current and contentious issue in your company. If the article is positive and praises your company, ring up customers to check if they are aware of the information and ask for their views on the piece. This allows you to test for any potential negatives from your audience to the activity and to take steps to respond to them.

Your employees may also be able to supply you with good PR material. During the course of their conversations with customers they may be able to identify PR situations which could help you promote your own company. If your customers are themselves interest-worthy, some of that interest may be conferred on you as a supplier. If your customer has had particularly excellent service from you he may be willing to allow himself to be used as a testimonial to encourage non-users to try you. You may be aware of your 'major customers' but it's often the smaller businesses who provide the most interesting stories.

Staff communication via the telephone

112

'We may only discuss the weather but I talk to every one of my senior managers every day. It's part of an understanding that I'm there for them and they have to be there for me. We talk face to face only once every five or six weeks so if we didn't have that telephone contact it would be very difficult to maintain that management team spirit and level of communication. In the time I've been here the team spirit has developed and worked very well. I would say the telephone is the most important tool in making that team spirit happen. The fact that you always take their calls makes them feel important – if you don't take calls from customers or staff, they feel they're not important enough for you to bother with them. Managers who are 'in meetings' or 'on the other line' don't build good communication!'

Internal calls between members of staff are unfortunately not always given the full attention and quality commitment that is desirable. The telephone helps to create a department's image, particularly if it is distant or remote from colleagues, or where the staff may never actually meet. In this case telephone manners are key indicators to employees about the effectiveness of that department. If you speak to staff about such departments you will realise that telephone communication is high on their list of gripes or praise. Phones which are not answered quickly, bored and indifferent tones, over familiarity or flippancy, lack of action in fulfilling telephone requests all contribute to a negative image.

Explain to your staff that such images are possible to establish themselves about your department if they do not have a total commitment to good telephone communication.

Another important factor is the role of the telephone in helping a manager to maintain close contact with his staff, especially if they only meet once a month or so. Memos and company papers or newsletters are limited as they do not allow any input or discussion from the employee. A telephone call is much more personal and allows your staff extra opportunities for one to one communication. If your staff meetings are with more than one employee, this is probably the only time an employee can enjoy your undivided attention apart from formal reviews or appraisals. The privacy and intimacy of the telephone can also encourage staff to be more forthcoming and such conversations may be very illuminating. If you cannot see as much of your staff as you would like, pick up the telephone. Not only will this help you to keep up to date and informed about what is happening in the business, it is very motivating for your staff. It also demonstrates your commitment to give them the support to which they are entitled from a manager.

113

When your staff ring you, be available every time if you possibly can. Being asked to leave a message with your secretary is very offputting and, if it happens often, demoralising. Taking the call is motivating because it confers status on the caller.

Showing your willingness to take the call also demonstrates to your staff that this is a standard for all if you ascribe to it. If you hide from the phone, so will they! Accessibility not only of yourself but of all your fellow managers and employees will help to percolate throughout your company the right attitude to the telephone as a medium of communication. You will also help to avoid the misunderstanding that can occur when somebody misinterprets a written request from you. The call will allow both parties to check their understanding of any action that is required of them.

RUNNING A TELECONFERENCE MEETING

Running a teleconference meeting is just like any other meeting. However, there are a few extra points which are worth noting: circulate any written documents in advance; provide an agenda explaining what you expect to achieve during the meeting – this is very helpful; check that each participant is in a quiet location – background noises can be distracting; introduce all the participants at the start of the meeting; address your comments to a **named** individual – no one can see you!; compensate for lack of eye contact and body language signals by checking regularly that people are happy with the progress and outcome of the meeting.

Using the telephone to negotiate

'It may be the negotiations begin with a letter and you respond with a letter. They may write again and you might decide at that point that a telephone call would be a better means of response. A letter will cost about £9.00 to send and perhaps the matter can be settled with a five minute telephone conversation.'

One of the major advantages of negotiating by telephone is the flexibility it offers you. Offers or suggestions made in writing have the big disadvantage of not being flexible. Using the telephone to negotiate indicates a willingness to arrive at a solution. A manager may be tempted to hide behind the comfort of the written word. You can check the contents with colleagues and polish up the phrasing before you put the letter in the envelope. But it does lead to protracted negotiation which can lead a customer to feel that he is not being dealt with satisfactorily. The time span of four or five days between letters wouldn't be unusual but it can be an awfully long time to a customer who is feeling badly done by.

Of course all kinds of negotiations can take place on the telephone, not simply those which involve arriving at a solution where perhaps one party is aggrieved at the actions of another. You can negotiate terms and conditions on a contract: you can negotiate the price you are willing to pay for something. The point about negotiating by telephone is that it allows both parties to explore verbally the range of options available to them, it allows you to try out various suggestions but without having to keep to that commitment because you have made the suggestions in writing. People will feel more free to comment on how realistic your expectations are if it is as part of a conversation.

One point about negotiating by telephone is that it does allow you to remain in control. A good technique for negotiating by phone is to make your offer and then remain silent. Leave it to the other party to come back to you. A telephone call is extremely effective for doing this as silence on the phone is somehow 'louder' and carries more impact than in any other situation. To demonstrate this point, listen to a tape recording of yourself on the telephone. Listen to the gaps in the conversation. You will be surprised to find that only a few seconds seems an awfully long time. Remaining silent forces your listener to fill the void in the conversation and respond. His response will give you clues about how he is feeling and whether he is going to accept your negotiating stance. The first one to speak loses!

Speeding up the response

'It was Christmas Eve and the phones were very quiet because business isn't always very good on Christmas Eve. The phone rang and I picked up the call. It was the purchasing manager of a conveyor belt company. They had just been bought out by a Swiss company and the deal had just been completed that very morning. As part of the deal they were required to contract hire vehicles. They were looking for five vehicles and they needed to get prices and complete the deal that day. They had contacted four or five other contract hire companies and the response they got was, well, minimal, to say the least. Firstly, a lot of companies were insisting on sending a field sales person in to see the company before they even began to quote. The difficulty for this company was that, as part of their deal, they needed to put pricing together for contract hire and they needed to do it there and then. So because of the quick response of telesales we were able to get the prices together very quickly and respond in an extremely efficient manner. This obviously impressed the company. Once we had given them the prices, we got the quotations together and we gave them the prices the same afternoon. It was then a case of how quickly we could get the vehicles. It was very important for this company to actually get the deal done as speedily as possible. There was no-one else – and they tried lots of other large companies who are market leaders – none of those companies had a telesales operation that was empowered to take the process through from the initial call to actually completing the sale. All these companies had a service whereby they would take the initial call and then arrange for a salesperson to go in, to quote – it was a long, drawn out process. No other company had the speedy response the customer needed. We were able to source the vehicles and we actually signed up the orders that afternoon.'

'Customers ringing in do not see the internal "machinery" and don't know what the person on the other end of the phone has to do to achieve the result. All they know is they rang first thing in the morning it's now late afternoon and there has been no response. It

115

can surely come unstuck if the internal customers isn't responded to with the necessary speed.'

Use the telephone to encourage your customers to contact you directly wherever possible. Using third parties such as external agencies diffuses your message and can lead to misunderstandings or lost opportunities.

Customers no longer work 'normal' hours. Part time work, job sharing, shift patterns and weekend working have all had an impact on businesses who may find it difficult to provide the sort of 24 hour coverage that may be required.

116

Give your customers at least the chance to leave a message, even if you cannot provide live staff to cover these unusual hours. It may be possible to pre-record messages that could answer specific enquiries and to provide operators to cover for exceptional calls only. As your customers find it increasingly important to have products or services available to them when they have the opportunity to make a call, it places increasing demands on businesses to cater for this need. The finance services industry has changed to accommodate this need and now direct banking by telephone is used by millions of customers who value its flexibility, friendly account management and instant response to requests for information, loans, overdrafts etc. This approach to business which is tried and proven in this area can equally be applied to other businesses.

Customers like to be dealt with immediately when they want to do business and they are not impressed with being asked to write, call back tomorrow or by any delaying tactic used by a company to try to get the customer to conform to their own work patterns.

'The other thing which is important is that if a customer or supplier has a problem and wants to speak to me, and it is a genuine molehill, if I don't get back to them for four hours it has developed into a mountain. It has developed in their mind and they've considered all the possible areas for disaster.'

Summary

Visits are a scarce resource, time consuming and expensive. Increasingly, companies are switching to using the telephone to maintain contact with their customers.

This principle also applies in other situations, eg a manager may not have the time to conduct one to one meetings with his staff, but a quick telephone call to update himself on the work in progress makes sense and still maintains personal contact.

Telephone conversations are shorter than in a face to face situation, and therefore less time consuming, but they still manage to convey your personal interest. You can control the call by making a list of the subjects you wish to cover prior to the call, and by sticking to that list.

It is also important to respond to what the customer needs. Many calls are made to businesses because customers simply do not have the time to involve themselves in lengthy correspondence. If they want to do business via the 'phone, so should you!

The telephone isn't a 'cure-all' designed to replace all written communication but it is worthwhile examining what possibilities are available to you for using the telephone instead. The telephone personalises your communication and has the extra advantage of being a two way communication between you, your customers, your staff and suppliers. Where possible, a written communication should be sent only to confirm and summarise agreement you have reached or action points that have arisen from the conversation.

117

How the telephone is good for business

Breaking the stereotype

How telephone selling created a poor image

If you are a manager who considers the telephone intrusive then you will almost certainly have reservations about using the telephone to maintain contact with your customers or indeed to sell your products or services. However, many businesses have been doing this successfully for some considerable time.

One of the problems has been that a number of companies have moved into telephone selling without being planned or organised about it and worst of all not ensuring that their employees have the training required to maintain an effective telephone service. Poor telephone selling standards when selling to the consumer have without doubt contributed to this poor image. For example, if you have ever had occasion to place an advertisement privately in your local newspaper, perhaps to sell a car or a piece of equipment no longer in use, then you will be well aware of how you are inundated with calls from rival publications, each anxious to assure you that theirs is the one which can achieve a sale for you. This is not only frustrating but also reinforces the bad image of telephone selling.

Recruitment advertisers are sometimes guilty of contacting employers who have placed recruitment advertisements almost on the day of publication. Clearly, common sense should prevail and it should be recognised that no employer is going to use a rival publication until at the very least he has the opportunity to assess the success or otherwise of his advertisement. Yet even today this practice still exists. It serves only to irritate and annoy and convince businessmen even further that this is a poor way to do business. For the businessman as a consumer, when he receives telephone calls into his home from people who do not have the necessary training seeking to sell products or services, not only does he consider this practice intrusive but again it reinforces his negative image of telephone selling in business.

It must be said straightaway that good telephone sales people are not cheap to employ. Advertisements in the press may lead you to thinking that you don't need to pay a good basic salary, for example, and indeed that telephone sales people are happy to work for commission only. But think about those calls you've had from the financial services sector – people trying to sell you insurance, or double glazing or kitchen equipment – or any one of a number of services. Most of these so-called sales people work on a commission only basis. They work on a numbers game – the more you ring the more likely you are of finding somebody who is interested. Whilst there isn't anything inherently wrong with this principle, the problem is that because they have so many calls to make, little or no time at all is devoted to training. Employers who consider commission only as a good means of remuneration almost certainly are not prepared to invest in training.

119

Telephone selling isn't necessarily cheap but it can be very effective. It can bring you huge rewards in terms of quality of service to your customers with the immediacy they have come to expect. When trying to cost the introduction of such an operation, include the benefits of retaining customers, providing a better service for them and compare it with the cost of a visit by a representative of your company. A typical reaction to introducing telephone selling into an organisation was voiced by one senior manager in the financial services sector. The company itself was a subsidiary of one of our main high street banks, who, incidentally, use telephone selling extensively, only they prefer to call it telephone marketing. He felt that his business would suffer from the introduction of telephone selling: that it had a down-market image which would reflect badly on his organisation. It transpired after conversation that his whole image and knowledge of telephone selling was limited to one telephone call that he'd received from somebody selling him, or at least attempting to sell him, kitchen equipment, someone had rung him late in the evening and had been extremely intrusive, starting off the call by pretending he was doing a telephone survey – a cheap tactic which guarantees a negative response from a potential customer.

Almost everybody who adamantly denies that they would ever allow a telephone conversation to take place with a sales person can be convinced if a call is handled well. So why not get somebody to ring them as a test case – or why don't you ring a company and ask to speak to a telephone sales person? If it is a reputable company you will almost certainly be very pleasantly surprised, although it is true that companies in general fail to appreciate that to maintain high standards of training and quality of communication it is necessary to revisit this subject time and time again. One-off training situations simply will not achieve this.

Think about calls that you may have made to book theatre tickets or holidays – or perhaps you've contacted hotels to see if accommodation is available. Have you ever placed an order with a mail order company or rung an information line? All of these are 'sales' situations. However, the chances are that you have only been struck by the efficiency and friendliness with which your call was dealt. This is essentially the difference between good telephone selling and poor telephone selling.

The misconceptions of the business community as to what qualities are required for good telephone sales people can be seen almost daily in recruitment advertising in the press. Look at the words that are used: aggressive – closer – determined – ambitious – all words guaranteed to create a poor image for telephone selling. I certainly wouldn't want to receive a call from a 'young ambitious closer' and I can quite see why businessmen wouldn't want to either. The point is that good telephone selling very rarely creates this sort of image. A call from a telephone sales person who is a good communicator should be a pleasant experience, something from which both you and the caller will benefit.

Telephone sales people don't want or need to sell to people who are not interested in their products and establishing this interest straight away is one of their prime functions. If you are totally uninterested in their proposition, they will go away and explore other avenues. After all, and this is a surprising thought for most businessmen, their time is as valuable as yours. It is only where people persist in pursuing the unpursuable or use dishonest tactics to gain access to you personally that this poor image becomes reinforced by such a negative experience.

Some years ago a telephone sales consultancy was featured in a television programme. The programme was specifically about selling. It featured field sales and telephone sales activity. It confirmed the worst prejudices of what constitutes a 'typical' telesales team. They were reinforcing the image that telephone selling somehow has to be accompanied by bells and whistles – that people have to induce themselves into an almost trance-like state to be able to get on the phone and talk to customers. The telesales person who got a customer to place an order or to agree to an appointment was greeted by loud claps and cheers.

This was not the enthusiasm of a well-motivated team and its poor values were confirmed later in the programme when it was revealed that people who had agreed either to buy a product or to an appointment later cancelled. A good telephone sales person would never allow such a thing to happen. When the telephone receiver is replaced, the customer should be sure that he has done the right thing. If he suffers post-call doubts he always has the opportunity to cancel. That is his right. In effective and professional teams this very rarely happens.

Customer contact programmes and total quality management

'When customers ring us, they expect us to have all the details of their account immediately accessible and for us to have a much greater knowledge about them than we actually do.'

The above is a comment made by the marketing services director of a well-established, medium-sized building society. It illustrates the gap that can occur between what customers expect and what a company can deliver. New technology which links customer databases to telephone systems allows you a great deal of sophistication and help towards solving the problem. They are, however, expensive to develop and have to be built over a period of time so they are not an immediate solution if you have no existing technology.

Although the building society could think of many reasons why it wouldn't be possible to have all the customer information it required to handle customer calls, the problem is that the customer could not think of one. Poor customer communications is your problem, not your customer's! The society had found itself in a classic dilemma. They had introduced a telecontact team to approach customers to discuss their financial needs with them and then found the team was less effective than it could be because they didn't have access to all the customer information they required to do the job well.

If you are in this situation you may have to resort to paper-based systems to help you if investment in the new technology is out of the question. At least it will give you the opportunity to measure the result of a contact programme before going further and investing in technology. Use customer record files. Insert in each file a 'call history' Fig. 7.1 which will include details of contact names, telephone numbers, addresses, what the customer currently orders from you, plus identified areas for developing potential business. Include the date you were last in telephone contact with the customer, who spoke to him, what was the reason for the call and the result of the conversation. Recording this information will help you to build information about the customer and his needs and wants so that you can contact him at the most appropriate time. If he has told you during the course of a conversation that he may be in the market for your products or services in a few months' time, agree a mutually convenient time to re-contact him and use your diary to record it.

Diaries are vital to ensure that opportunities are not missed. You should check desk diaries from time to time. If they are blank, somebody isn't doing their job properly because the customer cannot be getting a call when it was agreed that he should. Even electronic diary systems are open to manipulation. One manager said that the demands on his team were heavy and because of this, diaried customer contact calls were relegated to the bottom of his team's priorities. This is fine if it represents an occasional lapse but if it happens often, you may have a manpower problem. Diaried calls help you to contact the customer *when he wants to hear from you!* If you are not talking to your customers (writing to them isn't enough!) you will be out of touch with what they want from you.

One company had sales offices, service centres and operational depots plus an enquiry centre, all of which were heavily promoted to the customer. With no customer contact programmes in place, customer confusion was inevitable. The company has now introduced a proactive contact programme which has immediately identified a need to tackle this problem. TQM programmes must take telephone communication with prospects and customers into account or all your company's efforts to strive for quality will be lessened by poor verbal communication with customers, employees and suppliers. System changes are relatively easy to introduce. Attitude changes need creative management to achieve the best results.

CALL HISTORY

Contact name: _____ 1 ___

_____ 2 ___

_____ 3 ___

Tel. no: _____

Address: _____

_____

_____

Postcode: _____

		Jan	Feb	Mar	Apr	May	Jun	Jul	Aug	Sep	Oct	Nov	Dec
1992*	Vol	6		4	2					6	8	9	
	Rev	£100		£700	£150					£1,000	£1,400	£1,650	
1993	Vol	2	1		3								
	Rev	£400	£150	£500									

Date rung	Comments	Result
	– Record who was spoken to and the main subjects of conversation. *– If a problem is identified record action taken*	*Record outcome of call (order or diaried call back). Confirm the problem is resolved.*
	* Record details of customers spend with you to monitor fluctuations and identify trends.	

123

Fig. 7.1 An example of a Call History record

Introducing a telephone strategy

Before making strategic decisions, you need to establish how telephone communications work in your organisation or department.

Investigate the following:

- Who rings you?
- Who do you ring?
- What level of activity are the inbound and outbound calls?
- Have you got the right people at the end of the phone?
- Does your department service internal or external customers?
- Do you generate a lot of paperwork?
- How does internal communication work – is it via memos or telephone calls?
- What can you do to improve the current situation?
- Ask your customers what they would prefer?
- Is the telephone perceived as an intrusion?

Once you have established what you want to do to improve communications, define your objectives and identify the training and system gaps that need to be closed to help you achieve them.

Introduce your strategy in stages. Your employees are unlikely to make the quantum leap from 'Hello it's Smith speaking!' to a structured approach to the call using all the techniques available to counteract the lack of visual clues.

Try to involve your staff as much as possible in identifying where they can help to improve their performance on the telephone. Use the self evaluation sheets to help your staff to identify their training needs (Fig. 7.2) and the summary sheet (Fig. 7.3) to enable you to focus on group training needs. List the areas you want to evaluate in the 'key skill' boxes. It's easier to change technique than it is to change attitude but if you are clear about the direction in which you wish to go, at least you and your staff will start from a point of common understanding.

Your strategy should take account of the internal customers of your business as well as the external ones, particularly if you are trying to change the culture within your business. Put as much effort into developing the training skills of your employees who are not in customer

SELF EVALUATION – NEEDS ANALYSIS

Below are some key skills. As honestly as you can rate your ability on a scale of one to ten. The more confident you are of your ability the higher the score you should award yourself.

Key skill	Score

NAME:
DATE:

Figure 7.2 Self evaluation – needs analysis *(insert the key telephone skills that are appropriate to your business)*

E

SELF EVALUATION SUMMARY SHEET

Key skills			Names of staff entered here				

Scores entered for each member of staff alongside relevant skill area.

The completed matrix will help you identify urgent training needs i.e. where a preponderance of numbers cluster around 1–5.

Figure 7.3 Self evaluation summary sheet

facing departments because their skill and attitude on the telephone will impact on those who do speak directly with customers.

Your strategy should also focus on the non-sales or marketing areas of the business. Specialised telecontact teams do need extra training resources but it is foolish to rely on instinct, good manners or a few simple rules such as 'A telephone must be answered within three rings' to achieve telephone excellence elsewhere in the business.

Objectives could be to:

- Increase customer satisfaction.
- Make your department a 'one-stop' call.
- Reduce paperwork.
- Be more accessible to customers and employees.
- Project the right image of your company's aims and values in all telephone communication.

127

The use of external agencies versus internal resources

External agencies are almost always used where a company feels they do not have the internal expertise to manage a telephone resource. An external agency can bring you considerable experience and different ideas, particularly if they have been involved with other businesses similar to your own. However, the successful use of an external agency depends on the following factors.

Firstly you must be sure of what you want to achieve from your team. A poor brief to an agency will produce poor results. What you need to do is to sit down and plan the objectives of the campaign together. Look at the sort of script you want to use (a script should only ever be used as a prompt), the timescales involved and how easy it will be for a customer to respond to your marketing activity. One of the frustrating aspects of using an external agency is that when your prospective customers respond, they may in fact be in the mood to buy and all your agency can do is pass them on to you or to deal with only one aspect of the call. This can result in a wasted business opportunity.

Secondly it is important to ascertain just what experience the agency has and if, indeed, they have the resources to cope with the volume of calls you may expect. Front line people in an agency can give a gloss which may be misleading. Even better, ring up the agency as a prospective customer and analyse how they deal with the phone call. Did they sound warm and inviting? Were they efficient? Did they sound knowledgeable? In other words, did they give the sort of impression that you would want your own company to give? Always ask for references and always follow them up. It is amazing what other customers of an agency can reveal. Even if they have had an excellent service from the agency you need to be sure that your brief is similar to what their requirements were.

A final point is that agencies can be expensive and the cost of a call could be prohibitive if your company is a fairly small one. You may decide that you are better off doing it yourself. There is no doubt that external agencies have their place. They can be a useful bridge for a company taking on a commitment to introduce telephone contact in a more substantial way. They do have experience and they can help and advise on things like recruitment and telephone systems. The biggest disadvantage that agencies have is that they can never, no matter how much they may tell you or how much they try to convince you otherwise, bring to your company the commitment and enthusiasm of your own staff. It is this single factor which has persuaded many companies to bring their telephone activities in-house.

128

SUMMARY

The advantages of using external resources are:

- Agencies can be of benefit using their past experience to help you start a telecontact programme.
- They can help you set and achieve objectives.
- They can provide you with resources on an *ad-hoc* basis.
- You can 'trial' different projects without expensive investment.

Disadvantages are:

- Your customers are one step removed from you.
- You could waste opportunities.
- They can be expensive: handling costs per call will have an element of profit for the agency built in.
- Even with the most comprehensive briefing from yourself, their employees will not have the same knowledge of your company that your employees have.

POINTERS FOR CHOOSING AN AGENCY

- Check their knowledge and experience – does it relate to your needs?
- Does their recruitment criteria match your own?
- Ask for references – and follow them up.
- 'Mystery shop' – ring the agency and find out for yourself what your customers will experience.
- Establish that they have the resources to deal with the volume of calls you expect.

Banish the fear, gain the commitment

- Approach the task using the step approach, eg making sure a call is answered takes priority over how it is answered.
- Consider the impact that introducing a more pro-active telephone approach to customers may have on other employees.
- Always communicate what you are seeking to achieve. Say what you are doing and why. Brief your employees about changes and give them the opportunity to contribute their ideas and opinions.

129

Shy or nervous people may not be happy about being subjected to close scrutiny when on a telephone call so you will have to build up their confidence. An effective way to gain commitment is to encourage open discussions as to how they can improve. Help them to recognise poor performance in others – discuss calls from other people to the department or calls they have made to other organisations – once they are able to recognise poor performance in others they will be better equipped and more motivated to address their own shortcomings.

Always pass on any praise you are given by others about your staff and the way they handle a call.

USE THE STEP APPROACH

- Each call is answered quickly.
- The greeting conforms to your corporate image.
- The department is a one-stop call.
- Customers can contact anyone in the business easily.

- Records are kept up to date.
- Opportunities for additional business are identified.
- Customers get the information they need.
- Negotiation skills are improved.
- All aspects of the customers relationship with you are covered by appropriate training material which is available to assist staff.
- Your staff can handle any telephone situation.

It is difficult to leapfrog so take time to set each step in place before moving on to the next one. Motivate staff who are fearful or resentful by taking every opportunity to demonstrate your commitment to the programme and your willingness to change your own attitude and telephone manners. Start by accepting that call just when you were about to tell your secretary you were unavailable!

130 'People like to do business with people who like to do business with them'

One of the biggest potential areas for losing business starts with a very simple straightforward request. Potential or existing customers ring a company and ask for information about that business to be sent to them. This straightforward request is fraught with danger if, as in the case of large companies where such activity is generated as a result of extensive mailing campaigns, this task is often contracted out and telemarketing agencies are used to conduct the 'fulfilment' of such requests. The difficulty here is that when customers ring, they are not speaking to employees of the business which can lead to problems if the customer wants to discuss his enquiry in more depth, directly with the company. In addition to this, many companies remunerate their agencies according to the lengths of calls. This means that the more complex conversations, other than confirming a few basic details such as where the customer saw an advertisement, are actively discouraged.

If the volume of response is high, calls to the business may be 'lost'. Customers don't like to have to queue for an answer and may not call back. A constantly engaged tone is also offputting. Their calls may even be re-routed to a central enquiry facility and, where this is not automatic, being asked to ring another number is both irritating and unwelcoming. Worst of all, failure to send out the required information results in customers feeling let down and thus their opinion of your company will be a negative one.

Treat incoming enquiries like gold – think about how much money your company has spent trying to attract them.

Some organisations are reluctant to follow up such requests for information or quotes because they feel the customer may perceive this as being intrusive, if not a little pushy. This fear arises from a lack of understanding of how a well trained person can create the right kind of environment in which such a conversation can be developed towards a commitment from the customer to do business without them ever feeling that they have been harassed. If it is handled correctly, there will only be a warm acknowledgement of the friendliness and helpfulness with which the query has been dealt.

It may be part of your own experience that a company has rung you with a view to taking your initial enquiry a little bit further along the road. You probably felt pleased that they took an interest in doing business with you. Customers like to feel valued. They certainly don't like to feel that their business is being taken for granted and if they are a long established customer, a supplier is complacent about that situation continuing indefinitely. Companies who undertake a customer contact programme are pleasantly surprised by the reaction from the customer. Almost invariably they see it as an enhancement of the service that already exists.

131

A key factor in the decision to use a company is that the customer is influenced by the way in which his enquiry has been dealt with, and if a quote is sent out, why not discuss the customer's reaction to the quote by telephone? You are only demonstrating that you care about gaining that customer's business. Just as importantly, you will be talking to your customer during his decision-making process which will give you the opportunity to answer any questions or allay any doubts he may have.

- Failure to respond to a request for information creates a negative impression.

- Non-sales enquiries should be given equal care and attention – they influence your customer's perception of you.

- Don't be afraid to follow up requests for information or quotes – you demonstrate your interest in the customer.

- Reinforce your existing relationship with your customer by ringing him – don't always wait for him to ring you.

Customers like to be phoned

Where customers may have been doing business with you for many years and their only contact is via a field sales executive, a problem can occur in that the field sales executive may only have limited time to devote to such issues as customer service and account management. No matter how committed he is, the constraints on the time available to him will almost invariably mean that his actual contact with the customer is infrequent and more likely to be reactive, that is he will return a phone call from the customer, rather than pro-active. Unless you have a huge sales force, you cannot possibly hope to look after that business efficiently relying solely on a field sales resource and more and more companies are recognising that the field sales executive is more productively employed in seeking new business opportunities rather than retaining existing business. Therefore, if contact with your customers is infrequent, for whatever reason, the telephone can help you to bridge that gap. Your calls to a customer should always have an objective, so be clear about what those objectives are. When you ring the customer, tell him why you are ringing and what you hope to achieve from the conversation.

132

Customers will welcome opportunities to do business if they feel that the proposition is well thought out and worthwhile. If you have the right quality of personnel on the telephone, it can only be a pleasurable experience for the customer to be contacted by you. It gives him the opportunity to talk freely about what he wants and needs from your business and from the services or products you offer. By giving the customer an opportunity to voice doubt or opinion and by listening to what he says and acting on it, you are actually developing the relationship. There is no need to be nervous about speaking to your customers. If the call is approached in a friendly, professional way it will be welcomed. Such calls, in addition to helping you to develop your relationship with a customer, also give you the chance to increase the volume of business you are doing with them. You have an advantage that you must already be doing something they like – find out what it is and build on it!

If you do come across negative reactions from your customers, make a note of them and respect their wishes. The telephone is one of many communication options open to you. Find out which one works for your customer and use it.

- Your sales force may be 'new business led' and therefore reactive, rather than pro-active, to the needs of existing customers.

- Customers perceive your call as a commitment to service.
- It gives them the opportunity to discuss needs and wants.
- The call bridges the time gap between visits.
- Don't be disappointed if you unearth problems: it gives you the opportunity to put things right.
- Your call builds up the relationship between you and your customers.

Pro-active calls – customer service and the business opportunity

The telephone is used extensively in business (20 billion telephone calls each year). Therefore it is a reasonable assumption that it is 'good for business'. The issue is, 'Could it be better?'. Most managers will agree that much of their time is consumed by general administrative tasks, and certainly administration overheads are the least popular costs for any accountant. Managers are constantly looking for ways to reduce these costs, and an increasing number of companies are investing heavily in technology to achieve this.

133

A good example of this is mail order companies. Agents previously had to complete complex order forms and return them by post. Orders were then processed by clerical staff and when products were unavailable the agent had to be notified. All this took time and was very unwieldy. Today, the whole process has been computerised, and a bank of tele-operators are available (in some cases for 24 hours a day to accommodate shift working patterns) to take a telephone order, give instant confirmation of availability and to process an order for despatch in a very positive way. Free from the burden of form-filling, agents view the process as being more customer friendly and efficient.

Intriguingly, only very recently have the market leaders in mail order begun to experiment with more pro-active telephone contact with their agents. Even the most experienced companies (and the mail order market leader handles a volume of telephone calls second only to BT!) are only now realising the truth behind the concept 'people like to do business with people who like to do business with them'. Customers will not usually have a negative response to a company with whom they already do business, rather they will see such pro-active moves as a customer service and applaud the initiative of the company concerned. Whilst the reader may not be involved in such a business, the lessons are still valid.

Every call into or out of a business is an opportunity. The way in which telephone calls are handled should not be limited to basic telephone skills such as 'how to put a customer on hold'. Learning to communicate effectively using the telephone, combined with an alertness to opportunities, will increase ability to maximise the potential of every call.

Negative attitudes to calls should be discouraged. Your customer's only experience of your company, once he has decided to do business with you, may be via the telephone. Turn on your employees to the power of the phone because not only can you **do business** but, if the call is not handled well, you can **lose business.**

134 Telephone networking

All managers find themselves in the situation of being required to provide business information. It could be on any of the following:

- Market information/trends/activity.
- Competitor activity.
- Customer reaction to change.
- Changes to professional or statutory regulations.
- Staff relations.
- Implications of reaction to proposed changes in working practice.
- How to get the best out of new equipment.
- To get details of other companies' experience in specific situations, eg the introduction of a telecontact team.
- How Total Quality Management works in practice.
- What your customers and suppliers need or want from your business.

The above list is by no means exhaustive but it does give a good idea of how much information needs to be sought by a manager. Professional associations, agencies, other colleagues in the business, and trade magazines will help to keep managers informed and up to date but this is where telephone networking can be invaluable.

When was the last time your opinion was sought and you refused to give it? Use the telephone to identify sources of information in your business or industry. Even people who work in competition with you are forthcoming when approached. This is because, like you, they welcome the opportunity to check out what others are doing and welcome approaches for their opinion because it is flattering to be asked. Written requests are less advantageous for two reasons – people may never get around to replying and such a request is more formal and therefore more inhibiting. It checks the desire to help. The phone is a more spontaneous and less inhibiting approach as well as being more direct. Most businesses are only too pleased to tell you about the good things that are happening in their organisation and are willing to share their experiences with you.

Telephone networking helps you to keep in touch with managers in organisations all over the country and allows you to 'meet' more regularly than attending seminars organised by your professional associations. It also helps you to form a closer bond with suppliers or customers who are far flung and therefore not easy to meet regularly.

135

Summary

The question of whether the telephone is good for business is often coloured by the adverse reaction to the phrase 'telephone selling' (or marketing) from senior managers in the business. Whilst external agencies can provide indicators to the viability of including telephone marketing in your company's strategy, they can never bring the enthusiasm, knowledge and commitment of your own staff.

Introducing a telephone strategy to your employees would appear to be a fairly straightforward and non-controversial decision, but there are many implications which need to be considered. A change of attitude is required to achieve an instant and professional response to a telephone call, and creating a culture which treats telephone calls as business opportunities does not happen instantly.

Creative use of the telephone will achieve cost savings in some areas but this should not be your sole criterion. Customers value the immediacy of access that the telephone gives them. Calls may be made impulsively (a letter is a much more considered action). Your company needs to be able to offer an immediate response to a request from a customer in order to capitalise on this business opportunity.

8

The telephone web

How to avoid your customers getting caught in a contact trap

The impact that non-customer facing departments can have when they use the phone

It is true that many organisations are now devoting a great deal of time and attention, not to say money, on developing the telephone skills of their customer facing departments, for example, sales or customer service. Almost no attention is given to other areas of the organisation that may have an equal impact. Obvious areas are the finance department – credit control – accounts. Or perhaps a parts department or the department that's responsible for placing orders on your behalf. Administrative or clerical functions are very rarely given the opportunity to develop telephone skills, and yet all of these people are constantly using the telephone every day, either internally or externally. (Fig 8.1). Your customers may be impressed by the quality of your sales force but that good impression will diminish when they have an accounts query that takes a long time to sort out. Firstly, because nobody in the organisation knows who should be dealing with the query and then when they are put through to a department a long time elapses before the phone is picked up. Eventually they may succeed in making a connection with someone in your organisation who may not be willing to deal with the query by telephone.

Time and time again, the words 'please send it in writing' or 'if you care to write we will try and sort it out' are used to replace any real effort on an employee's behalf to solve a customer problem. Even sophisticated organisations are capable of coming out with such wild statements as 'I'm the only one here today. Everybody's out. Can you ring back on

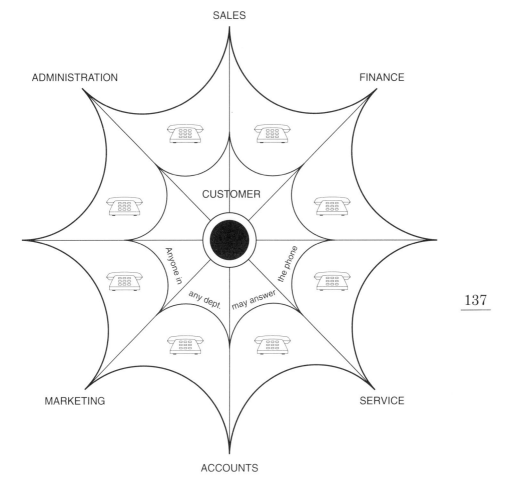

Some of the people a customer may contact when talking to a business

Fig. 8.1 Customer contact web

Monday and someone may be able to help you.' Or 'I'm sorry I have no idea who would have that information for you. The trouble is this organisation is so big we really need someone who knows what everybody else does, but I'm afraid we don't.' (This was said by an employee of the market leader in telecommunications!)

The people who took these calls were not unwilling to help. They simply did not have the skills or information to be able to deal with the call correctly. Many departments which have been considered to be non-customer facing in fact deal with and take calls every day, but they are frequently excluded when it comes to training in telephone skills. However, if a customer rings an organisation and is told that his query hasn't been dealt with because somebody has lost his fax or the post is slow, or the computer has broken down, they receive a negative impression of your organisation, and these are precisely the sort of comments that all too frequently are made by staff who are unaware of the impact that their words are having on customers who ring them.

One MD said that as a first step he would be happy to encourage his employees simply to pick up the telephone. The skills could follow later. This is true. Consider for a moment the occasions when you've made a telephone call. The speed of response at which the call is picked up at the switchboard level can be impressive but once you are then transferred to another department, the ringing out of a telephone can be extremely frustrating. You are in that awful limbo land, no-one is answering your phone, but you have made a connection to the company and you are paying for this call. Such negative impressions don't get good communications off on the right foot. Once you have addressed the problem of encouraging people to pick the telephone up and introduce themselves with your chosen corporate response, you then need to develop their skills further – how they handle the call and what they actually say both represent an image of your organisation. It is your responsibility to see that this image is a positive one.

138

The people behind the phone

Regardless of the size of an organisation, its efficiency can be judged in the way departments interact with each other and with colleagues in the same department. Almost everyone has uttered the words *'but I've explained all this to XXXXX. Didn't she tell you?'* It's frustrating, isn't it!

Powerful images are projected to callers when they ring an organisation. A company can weave a communications net which, without a proper telephone strategy, can only leave the customer feeling angry and frustrated – feelings he very rarely shares with you, he simply goes elsewhere.

Everyone can tell the mood of a friend who calls, simply from one word. A simple 'hello' can elicit the response, 'You sound cheerful' or 'You sound awful'.

If only one word can convey such meaning, think how much is deduced from a whole conversation. People's moods can influence inflection in their voices and change the whole meaning of a message they wish to convey.

A bored voice which thanks you for calling says as much about your department as it does about the person who picked up the phone. Because the people behind the phone are anonymous, the caller ascribes their attitude to your whole company.

An unanswered telephone conveys all kinds of messages: too busy, disorganised, uncaring, inefficient, and so on. Yet employees still perceive a ringing telephone as an intrusion into their working day. Some may even switch on an ansaphone while they are at their desk. I can imagine that there are some readers who do not see that as such a terrible thing. After all, managers are busy people, their day already filled without intrusive, unexpected telephone calls interrupting it. It is precisely this perception that needs to be changed. A telephone call should ultimately *reduce* the demands on your time if the call is dealt with properly.

139

A manager needs to create a culture where a ringing telephone is welcomed as an opportunity to do business, whether it's an internal or external customer. A colleague who asks a question or requests information or a solution will be far more effective if his call is dealt with properly. The satisfactory conclusion of a call can only enhance your employees' reputation and your department's and, ultimately, your company's image.

Most people who work in departments that are not used to talking to customers directly are very inhibited when it comes to picking up a telephone. Their reluctance to pick up a telephone may not be as a result of laziness or lack of interest, but a real fear of being unable to handle the call well. This is particularly true of people who pick up a telephone when visiting another department. The experience can be disorientating and even the most skilled managers and their employees may feel a little at a loss if they take a telephone call in these circumstances. What we need to do is to look at what people's inhibitions really are. Find out what it is they like and don't like about taking a telephone call. Once we can analyse these training needs we are then in a good position to develop their skills and write a training plan that will help them to overcome their problems.

The following is an account of how a newspaper proprietor who had recently acquired a major national newspaper rang the composing room just as the paper was about to be 'put to bed'. He demanded changes to the front page editorial and flew into a rage when he was told it was too late to do so.

'Do you know who you are talking to?' he screamed.

'Yes – do YOU know who you are talking to?"

'No – I don't . . .' came the by now slightly hesitant response.

'Well then, you can XXXXXX!!!'"

The phone was then slammed down, leaving the proprietor speechless.

It may be apocryphal but this story illustrates very well the freedom a telephone can sometimes confer on your employees to say and do what they like. This may result in someone being less than willing to help a customer and also they don't have the same sense of imminent danger that they would in a face to face situation, the danger being of course that the customer might make some demands on the employee's time which he is, at that moment, unwilling to give.

If your staff are genuinely reluctant to get involved with developing the company's telephone strategy you need to analyse why this is so. Perhaps it is because they don't have the right telephone skills, or it may be because they don't have the same psychological approach to a telephone call as they would in a face to face meeting. If they are really appalling in a telephone situation then you may need to consider whether they should ever be allowed near the telephone at all.

How to avoid your employees perceiving the telephone as an intrusion

A lot of internal strife within organisations is sparked off by the indifference with which internal telephone calls are treated. Somehow it seems less important if it's 'only' another member of the organisation who is ringing. The need to answer a telephone quickly and efficiently suddenly evaporates. Yet how your department interacts with other departments can be crucial to the successful running of a business. No-one operates in isolation. Too often members of staff can be seen talking to each other over the sound of a ringing telephone.

The telephone is intrusive because it demands an answer. The sound of a ringing bell can very rarely go on for any length of time being ignored. Perhaps it is because of this imperiousness that employees feel less willing to deal with the opportunity that is now presenting itself. People like to do things in their own time, not when they have been forced to do so as a result of someone else's actions – ie calling up on the telephone. It would be nice if all our customers and everybody else chose to write to us and we could then deal with each letter in turn, but customers today are far more impatient than this. They are used to the speed of response that telephones and computers allow. If a customer rings it is almost certainly because he requires immediate attention. If it was something that could wait for a written response, he would surely have written, wouldn't he?

Whilst it may be comfortable for your staff to demand everything in writing, this is no longer practical or feasible. If anybody in your department has ever uttered the words 'I feel as if I haven't achieved anything at all today, the phone just didn't stop ringing. I haven't had the opportunity to do my job' then almost certainly something is wrong with the way calls are being perceived or directed within the company. If the job is such that total unbroken concentration is needed, perhaps then you need to look at why calls are coming through to this individual. Or it could be because he is so willing to take ownership of the call that colleagues allow this to continue to happen and put all incoming calls through to him.

141

The use of a tick sheet can determine who in your department takes the most incoming calls. It isn't always desirable to have one individual who takes all incoming calls if it means that their performance elsewhere in the job is affected. It may even be that they have problems with certain aspects of the job and are using the incoming calls as an excuse to avoid facing these issues. Or it may be that this particular individual handles the calls so well that you need to look at passing out whatever it is that is not being completed to other employees in the department.

It could also be that telephone calls are taking up a disproportionate time of the working day because the calls are not being handled properly. A skill analysis should help you focus on the training needs of your staff and it should also help them to deal with the telephone call in such a way that a positive result is gained and it does not lead to a request for further written material which in turn will add to the paperwork.

An indicator of the attitude change required is a comment from an accountant of a large company, which was a market leader in its field.

Whilst it had only 300 employees, it did have 50,000 customers, any one of whom was likely to ring the company with a query. Despite the relative smallness of the company in terms of its employee base, the complex nature of its business meant they had a constant problem with mis-directed calls. Anyone in the company was likely to find himself talking to a customer.

However, this particular accountant, an expert in his field (company taxation), felt that as he had two staff working for him whose sole purpose was to shield **him** from **customer queries**, any attempt to improve the way calls were handled need only be addressed to his staff. This was not his speciality and therefore was irrelevant to him. His comment during a discussion was 'I don't see why this should involve me'.

The point here is that the way calls are handled is the responsibility of everyone in a company who has a telephone on his desk. Calls from colleagues need to be treated with the same degree of attention as external calls and anyone with a telephone should recognise that if the phone rings and you answer it, you need to be prepared for anything you hear.

A manager's attitude to handling calls will colour that of his staff. Staff will not show commitment if a manager feels that telephone calls are unwelcome.

Setting standards

Whilst answering the telephone quickly is important, even more important is the way in which the call is handled. Did the person who took the call sound friendly, enthusiastic, willing to help? Was their knowledge of your department and its function within the business good enough to answer a query satisfactorily?

Make a list of the things you think your people need to know. Analyse the type of calls they get and what information you think they need to be able to deal with calls satisfactorily. From time to time, make calls into the department yourself and check how they are being dealt with. Ask your colleagues in the organisation to do the same and make sure there is an opportunity to feed back any criticisms, constructive or otherwise, that come to the fore as a result of these exercises. If people don't know they are doing things wrong, they will never take the steps necessary to put things right. Consideration needs to be given to the acceptable amount of time it should take for a telephone call to be returned. I would suggest that one hour is about right. If your department takes longer than this to return a telephone call, you are in danger of the caller ringing again. This is not only extremely irritating for the caller, but it casts a poor light on your department's willingness to respond to calls. No matter what tasks they are involved in, they should have the opportunity within an hour to return the telephone call.

When agreeing what action is to be taken as a result of the call, make sure that your employees use realistic timescales. They may be optimistic in suggesting to the caller that a solution or a decision can be reached that day, especially if they need to refer to an absent manager. Callers usually accept whatever is proposed if you explain the reason, so give realistic timescales. If you have given an undertaking to resolve a situation the same day and subsequently it goes over into the following day, this can have a negative effect on the caller. However, if as unavoidably these things do occur, a standard could be that a call is made before close of business that day to advise the customer of what is happening. Customers are usually more willing to accept delays when they have been advised that they are about to take place. If the call is held over until the following day without the customer being informed of the circumstances behind why this has happened, it only serves to remind the customer of the problems that he is currently experiencing with your organisation.

Leading by example

You need to convey to your own staff your willingness to take telephone calls. It is surprising how often managers complain about the way telephone calls are handled in their department and yet fail totally to set a good example. First of all, you should always be available, that is available to take telephone calls. It isn't good enough to say you are not able to take calls because you are busy. If the task in hand requires such a level of concentration, it is debatable whether you should be in your office at all. Perhaps a quiet place elsewhere would be more appropriate.

Managers are paid to be available, both to their staff and to their customers. One manager who rejoiced in the company title of Customer Services manager was heard to announce without a shadow of a blush to members of his department that he didn't have to take telephone calls from customers and whoever it was on the phone that wished to speak to him should write in if they felt strongly about something. If somebody who is paid to give good service to customers thinks like this, imagine how managers in finance, operations and service departments may feel!

Brief your secretary on putting calls through to you. If there are certain calls that you feel you absolutely do not want to take, she should be aware of what these are and how to screen them out and then be able to put the relevant calls through. It's very embarrassing explaining to a caller why a manager cannot come to the telephone and that catch-all phrase 'He's in a meeting' simply will not do. One manager in a company that employed 400 people screened himself totally from the bother of taking external or internal calls. This was incredibly frustrating for fellow managers in the business who needed to call on him for fairly quick decisions to enable them to solve customer problems. His staff so readily used this phrase that even if he had stopped by a colleague's desk for a momentary chat, callers would still be told that he was 'in a meeting'. Of course, what happened was this devalued his meetings to such an extent that people no longer believed that he was in one and unavailable.

144

Your telephone should be included as a part of the hunt group so that if everyone else is on the telephone, you take the call as a matter of course. Equally managers should not ignore the sound of a ringing telephone on one of their employees' desks. Don't be frightened to speak out and demand that the call be taken. Unless your employees see that you take the issue of ringing telephones seriously, you can never expect them to do so.

Use the corporate response yourself and make sure that your people do. If you are leaving the office tell your people where you are and how you can be contacted. Lots of managers use car telephones and there is absolutely no reason why, on a trip, you cannot still be available to your customers. Help reduce the mountain of paper by avoiding writing memos wherever possible. Use the telephone instead. Once your managers and employees see that you keep this general rule they will start to do the same and between you all you can effectively reduce the paper chase.

How telephone skills can contribute to your TQM programme

Harry Ewins is a Practice Management Consultant for Conquest Legal Marketing.

> **'TQM is a very popular phrase but unless it is built upon the foundation of good operating methods then it is something that is going to give everybody a bad name because as soon as someone identifies the client's needs through TQM analysis and they do it badly because they haven't put the operational guidelines in place, then TQM will just be "the thing that doesn't work". You must get your procedures working correctly so that you do things right and then use TQM to make sure that you do the right thing.'**

External customers ringing in to an organisation that hasn't paid attention to its communication processes with customers will almost certainly end up with very ambivalent feelings towards that organisation. Even the most sophisticated organisations who spend literally millions of pounds on publicity, advertising and mailing, somehow forget to include the telephone in the communication maze. Some organisations do offer basic telephone training and, whilst this is a start, it is by no means enough. It is no good being trained in how to take a message if you then do nothing with the message – or indeed, how to answer a call with a corporate response and then not listen carefully and hard enough to what the customer is trying to tell you.

145

As much attention also needs to be given to problems of enhancing internal relationships. Companies may have departments which need to interact with each other frequently. Perhaps your operations department needs to ring depots or your sales department needs to contact credit control, or the people who have to despatch goods. Almost every employee can think of a department within their organisation that they don't like to telephone either because the people employed there appear to be obstructive, or don't return calls, or don't act on things that have been agreed during the call. You need to ensure that it isn't your department that people are talking about!

If you are in the process of implementing a total quality programme, the last thing you need is departments not being able to communicate effectively with each other. The speediest way is by using the telephone. But how often do people give enough thought to their company's or department's image when they are on the telephone? If your employees need to take messages, then the mechanisms must be available to enable them either to pass the message on to the appropriate person or to take action themselves.

One of the main drawbacks to TQM in this country is that while the word 'empowerment' is used often and in some cases with a great deal of passion, the reality is a long way from the truth. The powers, for example, to negotiate are very limited and the company hierarchy asserts itself. The phrase 'I'll have to refer to Mr So and So' or 'I'm afraid I can't deal with that' all indicate that employees haven't got the level of empowerment required to do their job properly. Although these issues may be difficult to solve and may even be beyond your control, you can help by improving the way calls are handled.

Good telephone skills can enormously reduce the effect that such policies may have on your internal or external customers. Keeping your customers informed about what is happening, and why, will go a long way to increasing customer satisfaction levels. If the trouble is taken to convey warmth and enthusiasm this will have a positive effect on your department's image. It will make people feel that they have been treated fairly and properly and even if the call was to initiate a complaint, the way a complaint is dealt with says more about your organisation than any other single issue. Your products or services can be the best in the country but if you fail to deal with a customer query correctly, your customer base will diminish.

How to encourage your staff and colleagues to take 'ownership of the call'

Probably one of the most irritating things for both customers and employees is when someone fails to return a telephone call or when some action has been requested by telephone and the follow through fails to happen. For example you may ask for some literature to be sent to you and it fails to arrive, then you have to go right back to the beginning and start all over again, giving the same details to yet another anonymous member of the organisation. If you have failed to get the name of the person you spoke to, this means you have no idea who to contact so you can't even follow up the call by trying to take some action with regard to that particular member of staff's failure.

Ownership of the call simply means that whatever course of action you agree to take, you also take personal responsibility for making sure that it happens. One of the difficulties for a manager when addressing this problem is the lack of control he has. You cannot be present at every telephone call and are almost certainly not a party to the conversation that is taking place at the other end of the telephone. It is too easy to 'walk away' from the consequences of the call. Listed below are some of the actions you can take to try and overcome some of these difficulties.

- Always lead by example. If you are reluctant to accept telephone calls and act on them, this can only transmit itself to your staff as a tacit approval of this sort of behaviour. By demonstrating that you are willing to accept calls and by taking incoming calls yourself when the need arises, you will communicate a positive attitude to your employees.

- Set out the procedure you expect your people to follow in every instance.

- Make it easy for your staff to deal with telephone enquiries by ensuring that they are fully briefed in the activities of the department and changes that may be taking place in the business.

147

- Talk to your staff about difficulties they may encounter when dealing with telephone calls.

- Feed back to your staff examples of calls that have been well handled. If customers make favourable comments, make sure that these are passed on to your people. Everybody always appreciates praise and recognition of a job well done.

Do these phrases sound familiar?

'I was just passing.'

'I don't work in this department.'

'I don't know the person you are asking for.'

'I'm not sure who you should speak to.'

(and perhaps the most damning of all . . .)

'You've come through to the wrong department.'

This last is especially irritating precisely because it confers blame on the caller who, through no fault of his own but rather because of a switchboard operator guessing, is now stuck with someone who clearly wishes they'd never answered the telephone.

Remember, when someone answers a call they represent your department or company in whatever capacity the caller invests in them. Whilst it isn't practical for all employees to be able to answer every question that is directed to them, if the call is answered enthusiastically and willingly it will go a long way towards conveying the style and image you would wish.

Practical hints to improve your organisation's internal communication

One of the most frustrating things for someone who is trying to put a telephone call through to the right person is identifying which extension they may be contacted on. Even the most organised, well-equipped companies who have PC-based telephone directories can be faced with a situation whereby they cannot find the person they want to put a call through to. Your internal telephone directory needs to be well-maintained. Somebody in the company should be made responsible for ensuring that staff movements and newcomers to the organisation are included in the directory. Keep it as up to date as possible. Managers frequently change their staff around, perhaps moving somebody from one desk to another. They then forget to inform the switchboard and long after somebody has left a particular extension, calls may continue to be put through. Always report this back to the person nominated to maintain the directory.

Equally, company organisation charts need to be distributed regularly amongst your staff. Often companies are reorganising and restructuring and such changes are not always communicated effectively throughout the company. Whilst people in the affected departments may be well aware of changes, somebody who operates from a different branch or division, or even on a different floor in the same building won't always be completely aware of what is happening. Anybody who is likely to be affected by such moves should be kept up to date with the changes.

Where possible, try to develop a company handbook which will list each department and its function, tells you what they may be able to deal with, and includes each member of that particular department and their telephone extension. Customers are often frustrated by being put through to the wrong department because the person who took the call 'second guessed' which department ought to be contacted. You can help them to eliminate the need to guess by taking practical steps to enable them to make the correct decision about where the call should be routed. The handbook must be succinct and easy to assimilate. If it is too detailed, your staff may spend too much time reading the handbook before being able to give a proper reply to the customer.

Departments' activities frequently overlap – or it may be that you yourself have made incorrect assumptions about who does what. If this confusion is apparent when you tackle the subject, think how it may appear to the new employee, especially if your organisation is a fairly large one. The more you can do to make the company comprehensible to your staff, the more you will improve its internal and external communication.

Staff frequently get irritated by calls coming through to a department when they are unable to help. Of course, they can reroute the call but this simply compounds the irritation all round. A good example of this is a finance department. There may be people in the department who do not get actively involved in customer communication. Perhaps they are there to audit internal accounts and not get involved in invoice queries. If a customer or a member of staff has an invoice query, it is all too easy to put them through to 'somebody in the finance department' and think that you have done your duty, but unless they put them through to the right person in that department they are clearly failing. Therefore, the more effort that is put in to involving your staff in writing your department's contribution to the company handbook, the more you will help to minimise the problems that can subsequently occur.

149

You could also encourage pride in good communications amongst your employees by developing a league table. Draw up a list of the type of calls each department may take. Put together a call analysis sheet and involve your employees in making calls to each other's department, scoring the person who answers the call on the points you have identified. (You can use the call analysis sheet Fig 3.1 as a guide.)

By involving your employees, they begin to appreciate how important it is always to respond well to incoming telephone calls, and of course it's fun for them to be able to mark other people's performance. Don't hesitate to allow them to ring other managers in the organisation! You can then publish the results on a department by department basis. You don't have to name individuals, simply how each department scored. You can structure this activity by making the calls once a month or once a quarter, or whatever you think is practical.

Finally, publish these results in a league table. Perhaps a certificate can be awarded to the department that scores the highest number of marks, recognising their achievement and commitment to good communication. It could be signed, for example, by your company's own communications manager or whoever you think may be the most appropriate – a director of the company or manager of an individual department.

Always recognise your employees' efforts to improve communication. By doing so you will encourage them to greater efforts. It is hard work at first but as you go on you will find that it becomes self-managing. If it is recognised and accepted that these are the standards the company is looking for, the commitment to achieve them and ensure that they happen with every call will be strengthened by allowing your employees to see that you are actively measuring their efforts and will publicise the results.

150

When going through the score sheets do discuss with your own employees how the call was handled, if real problems seem to be occurring. You can also advise managers of the department you are ringing and they in turn can take it up with the employee concerned. In this way you are managing a situation but not inhibiting your employees' participation by naming individuals in a public way. The aim is to identify the problems and to help employees accept that they exist. Then you can work together to identify how you can best resolve the problems that have been highlighted.

Presenting a cohesive image to your customers

A situation can arise whereby the merits of presenting one telephone number to customers is compared with the merits of channelling calls directly through to the appropriate department. One organisation felt that because of the complexity and size of their business, to try to include all telephone numbers would be confusing to the customer. Therefore it made sense to have one freephone number which a customer could ring and, from there, be routed through to the correct department. The theory was fine – however, in reality this department already dealt with a huge number of incoming enquiries to the business from existing customers. By using this freephone number on advertising and pro-motional literature, they were encouraging prospective customers, whose interest had been stimulated by the mailing, to contact the department. Of course, the inevitable happened – they simply couldn't get through. So prospective customers' first impression of this company was that of a ringing telephone with nobody to answer it at the other end. The lesson is that if you are going to use the same telephone number on all your literature, do be sure that the department you are channelling the calls through to is equipped and has the resources to take the calls and deal with them promptly.

If the customer is paying for the call, you need to think very carefully about the practicality of the customer being someone who is perhaps based in Scotland being asked to ring a number in a southern region to further their enquiry. Naturally, if the call is being made during peak hours, customers will be reluctant to ring long distance and you may actually switch them off, so in this instance it is probably more practical to use the telephone numbers of regional branches or offices to encourage people living within that area to contact the regional office direct. Certainly regional sales offices prefer this approach. One manager said 'We have an office based in Scotland, yet our customers are directed to an office based in Buckinghamshire. Naturally they assume that we are not bothered about having a base in Scotland. Our customers prefer to do business with people who are in Scotland. We lose out on potential business because prospective customers feel we are not sufficiently committed to this area to run an office. It's crazy. We're here and we want to take calls but the company's strategy does not allow us to do so.' You can alleviate this problem by using a number which then re-routes the calls automatically to the sales office nearest to the source of the call.

151

Centralised switchboards can be extremely useful in quickly directing incoming calls to far-flung areas of the business. However, by their very nature, these switchboards are usually extremely busy. If your cus-tomer's conversation is likely to take longer than a few moments the operator may become agitated because she is aware of the number of calls piling up behind him. If your business faces this problem, you should consider setting up a customer help desk, using a number of people familiar with the business and with access to information which will help them deal quickly and efficiently with the query. Such help desks are useful in demonstrating to your customers that you are able to respond quickly to incoming enquiries in the appropriate manner and to re-route calls efficiently. This concept can be developed to actually allow the people on the help desk to deal with the queries themselves. In other words, they take ownership of the problem, so instead of your customers being faced with the prospect of being put through to different departments, the help desk undertakes to identify what information it is the customer requires and to call the customer back with an answer. This is an expensive option but if your company is service orientated and you want to give the best possible service to your customers, it is certainly worth considering.

Companies who are involved in a lot of outbound telephone activity very often cause confusion to the customer by not being properly organised themselves. For instance, sometimes mailing activities are duplicated or overlapped. If you then follow up such mailings with a telephone call, what can result is that your customer can receive several calls from your business within a very short space of time. He can only come to the conclusion that you don't know what you are doing or whatever it is you are doing isn't terribly well organised. Either way, it creates a negative image of your business. So try to manage outgoing activities in such a way that duplication is avoided. Have controls in place that will help you identify customers who have already received a mailing. Structure the mailing activity in such a way that no customer receives more than two or three communications from you per annum unless that communication is to announce a new product or service, when of course they will want to be informed about such developments. You can organise your outbound team in such a way that they are ringing your mailing list either alphabetically or geographically and this will help to minimise the duplication further.

A problem often occurs where, if you are mailing at branch level, your operators may be referred back to the same 'decision maker' and then it is very difficult to avoid duplication. It can be very upsetting for one of your operators to make a call to somebody and be told, in a very curt way, that they are the fourth or fifth person from your organisation to ring them. You can try to avoid some of the problems by taking the trouble to research your mailing list prior to the mailing activity. By doing this you will eliminate the possibility, as far as possible, of the same person being contacted a number of times, because list cleaning should enable you to identify the companies which are managed from one central source. You can then write directly to a head office and minimise duplication.

How to make your department a 'one stop' call for your customer

Employees who are working in what is known as customer facing departments, that is they deal with telephone enquiries every day from customers, are well aware of the importance of taking ownership of a call. That is because they are encouraged to do so and this awareness will form an integral part of their training. They understand that when a customer rings an organisation it is an opportunity to do business. If you are a manager in a non-customer facing department, this culture will probably have failed to percolate through to your employees. If you work, for example, in a marketing department it is unlikely that a customer will be routed through to you, but it can happen. Unfortunately if people in the department are not geared up to dealing with enquiries by telephone, they lack the experience which will help them to develop skills to deal with them. If it is an administration department where telephones are notoriously silent, somebody may feel that the ringing telephone is not an opportunity but an intrusion. It is this quality of intrusiveness that is probably the biggest single factor in failure to handle incoming telephone calls well. Usually, especially if the department is a busy one, the temptation to push the call to somewhere else is great.

153

So what can you do to encourage your employees to make your department a one stop call? If your employees don't usually deal with customers, they can be forgiven for thinking that they are a little bit put on: after all, they are being asked to do somebody else's work. In general, people are very reluctant to do this. However, it's the customer who is important and to help the customer you need to persuade your staff to see things from the customer's point of view. You can encourage your department by explaining why it is so important that they accept a call willingly and helpfully and why, even if the call cannot be dealt with satisfactorily by themselves, it is important to have the call returned to the customer from the company rather than asking the customer to ring elsewhere. It is so easy to pass on a telephone number, it's quick and gets rid of the problem but it isn't helpful to the customer.

If your employees are under pressure, they may say they are unable to complete a task because 'the phone hasn't stopped ringing all day'. But this is acceptable if they have dealt with those calls properly. When your customers want to speak to you, you must be prepared to speak to them.

Any other activity in the business has to take second place, and by encouraging your employees to think in this way you will enable them to recognise the value of this. Just as importantly you need to demonstrate your commitment to the concept. So if you are tempted to criticise when work may not be done on time for the reasons given above, *bite your tongue!!*

Summary

- Demonstrate your willingness to answer the telephone by doing it yourself if no-one else is available. Even if you are in a meeting, you can retain control of the call and therefore deal with the situation with the minimum of fuss and disruption.

- For employees in non-sales and marketing environments, you must take the time to explain the importance and benefits of improving their telephone skills. They may assume that a polite manner is enough – it isn't.

- TQM programmes, customer care or sales drives come to nothing if it is lunchtime and no-one is answering the phone, or if a temp has not been adequately briefed. If someone in a service department agrees to credit a customer who has been given a faulty part, does he fill forms out or does he pick up the phone? Does he know who to ring and is written communication vital?

- Customers don't know how your department works, and if your colleagues don't know either, there is a danger that your customer could become tangled in the 'contact web'.

- Anyone who is likely to ring your department should have a named contact, preferably an alternative one, too.

- Conduct a skill analysis of your employees. Consider the telephone situations they may find themselves in. What do they need to know?

- Do your staff inform the switchboard when calls are not put through to them correctly or do they simply allow it to continue?

- Use a tick sheet to determine the type and volume of calls you receive and construct a training plan to deal with them.

- Do everything you can to make your department a 'one stop call', ie your caller should be dealt with immediately. If he needs to speak to someone else, get them to call him back. Thus, you will go a long way towards alleviating the intense frustration felt by a caller who is passed from department to department.

- If this culture percolates through your organisation you will achieve the accolade 'Good people to do business with'.

155

9

How seven companies put 'power behind the phone'

How other companies have successfully implemented a telephone strategy

You've got the power!

The reader should by now be convinced that applying telesales experience in all his customer telephone communications should enhance the company's performance, both in sales results and quality of service to the customer. Having conducted your own telephone audit, all you have to do now is convince your employees that serious consideration should be given to the implementation of a telephone strategy.

To provide inspiration and examples, this chapter will use quotes from managers who have already started down this path, or may be in the process of doing so. Their comments will demonstrate to you their motivation and success in introducing a professional approach to the use of the telephone. This is an area of business activity which is seeing actual growth during the current recession.

David Moss – Personal Sector Director, Barclays Bank

BARCLAYCARD – SETTING UP AGENTS

We set up a recruitment line where instead of always having to send representatives out from a sales office when someone said 'could you come and see me?', as we had done previously, the central unit, using a screen based pc system, could input all the merchant details as they gave them over the phone and we could complete the transaction. This improved our turnaround time dramatically. We promoted the telephone number through local directories and by word of mouth.

The major benefit to us was that we could centralise the function, make it more efficient and pass on a lot of that efficiency to the customer. Before, the customer had to contact a sales office who would then contact the representative who covered that area and it would depend whether the representative was in that town today, tomorrow, or he might have been there yesterday and was not going to be back in the town for another ten days. We could now get the paperwork out to the customer the same day and speed up the whole process.

We started off with ten operators. It grew and then shrank again because we learnt a lot more about how we could link technology to the operation and improve the input process. When we started we were inputting data onto a screen and then we had to wait for a printer to print something off and there was a whole series of back ups necessary. What we did over a year was to link the process together so that when a conversation was finished the letters and pack were generated. When the retailer completed the application it was returned to another department to leave the people on the telephone free to deal with calls coming in.

157

The help line dealt with all queries and now we are at the stage to bring the two together to enable us to manage the flow of work. Queries peak first thing in the morning before the retailer is open. They peak again at lunchtime and then in late afternoon. Recruitment calls tend to come through mid-morning through to mid-afternoon so we can now balance the peaks and troughs. We started off with only basic equipment, eg headsets, and initially we had very little monitoring of calls in terms of managing the peaks and troughs. Gradually we used more technology so that we could measure the volume of calls in half hour peaks.

Another area where we use telephone lines extensively is in Barclays' card authorisation service. We are open 24 hours a day, 365 days a year, answering authorisation calls from merchants. We have banks of operators using a sophisticated call management system. Originally we were based in Northampton and then moved to Liverpool. We invested in technology to improve our service. The automatic call distribution system is now being integrated with our computer. The operator takes a call and keys in all the card details and accesses our authorisation computer system either for Barclaycard, Visa or MasterCard and we now want to link all those actions up as the systems currently 'stand alone' and we want them to 'talk' to each other. This will speed up our response drive to the merchant who obviously wants a 'yes' or 'no' quickly. What he doesn't want is 'Can you hold for 20 minutes while I work this one out?'.

Learning points

- Focus incoming sales enquiries on a group of people who are specially trained to handle them.

- A centralised function increases efficiency which you can pass on to your customers.

- Using the telephone enables you to give an immediate response to your customer. A field sales person may not be able to respond with such speed.

- Use technology to link your phones to your computer system.

158

BARCLAYS PHONE BANKING

We are also evaluating the use of the phone in other areas. As life changes and the way we bank, and the way we undertake our daily routine changes more and more people like the telephone as a medium for giving the bank instructions and speaking to us. Personally I've banked in London for ten years and only recently have I asked them to transfer my account to the North. I've always dealt with them by telephone and an increasing number of people want to do that. They have busy lives and can't get into the bank as frequently as they would like or they want a different option. We are trying to provide that option for our customers who want to telephone us.

If we send out a mailshot on a particular product or service, often it generates questions. We can't get everything into a mailshot and into a discussion about it. We want to make it much easier to resolve a lot of those questions. A face to face discussion is ideal but that is not always practical. If we can talk to people on the phone we believe it benefits both parties.

We do telephone our customers and for a number it's an appropriate thing to do. With a customer base the size of ours we cannot use the same approach with everybody. Some of our customers like to receive a call from us. Despite what everybody thinks the calls from us are welcomed and they like to discuss the possibilities of using new services. We might only ring to say 'is everything alright?'. Some may not like us to call and we try to satisfy the different ways our customers want us to communicate with them. Increasingly we are trying to develop different routes or channels to our customers because we need to make sure they are happy with the service they are getting from us and that they are aware of the services we provide.

One of the major problems for us is that despite advertising, despite everything else we do to promote our services, our customers are not always aware of the extent of our services. They may have stereotype views of banks and financial institutions and I presume it's the same for any other company. The more we enlighten them about what we can provide – some people are amazed when we say to them 'Do you know we do mortgages?' – the better.

Increasingly as people become more aware, as communication spreads they will look for the service, quality and price they wish to pay. I don't think that's any different for banks from any other company.

159

We try to speak to all our new customers soon after they have opened an account. To people who come in and open an account we will say that we will ring them in a month's time to check that everything is okay. We ring to ensure that they have got their cheque book and that they understand how everything works. We will bring into that conversation whether we have perceived any needs or ask if there is anything they need or want.

As we get to know the customer better we might think of a service that the customer would benefit from and we would contact him about that. We don't ring everybody but instead we try to target our calls to those customers who we think have a need. It's a waste of our time and our customers' time if we make calls that are not of interest or benefit to them. We have all had experience of randomly targeted calls and paramount in our minds is that the call has to be a 'quality' call. We don't want to call people who prefer us not to, but we do want to speak to people who are happy to receive a call and, most importantly, other calls in the future. We do have a duty of care in that field.

We have a unit called Barclayloan Direct which accepts incoming calls from people who want to borrow money. It's a facility whereby customers can phone from their own home or anywhere to discuss a loan, go through the procedure, get all the information they require and the loan can be sanctioned over the phone. The paperwork can then be sent to them. The call may be referred back to a branch if there is a particular problem. It gives our customers the additional facility so that if they come into a branch and it's busy, rather than wait they can contact us by telephone. They may even prefer to telephone if they are nervous about sitting in front of somebody. It's also convenient, eg if you have seen a car you like and you can't get to a branch or you don't want to go to a branch, from having seen the car, you can go back to your house and pick up the phone and talk to somebody about the loan. In a high percentage of cases you will actually get a sanction on the spot. For major purchases people like to discuss it as a family and that may be when the bank is closed. A customer may be frustrated if he wants to get things done, say at the weekend after coming home from Saturday shopping. Now he can ring the bank and get things sorted out.

The Consumer Credit Act does preclude us from calling a customer specifically to talk about credit. If a customer has opened an account and we have telephoned after a month to talk about it, we wouldn't discuss loans. If a customer did say he was thinking of buying a new car we would explain to him that we have products and services that may be of interest to him and suggest that he came in to see us at the branch, send him an application form or suggest that he phones Barclayloan Direct.

The staff in the telephone units receive specific telephone training and all staff who enter the bank receive on the job training on how to answer the telephone and how to transfer calls etc. One of the things we do increasingly try to pay particular attention to, as more and more people speak to us by telephone, is ensuring that we manage the process of answering the telephone and how we pass on the calls if we have to pass them on to other areas. That is something we focus on and it is subject to Customer Service levels we want to achieve in our quality programme. We use a central training department to train in the making of outward bound calls to customers and we have people who go out to branches and coach people on how to do it.

160

Learning points

- If your customers like to do business by phone you must change current practice to accommodate that.
- You can support your mailshot activities by making it easy for your customer to discuss questions they may have.

- Target pro-active calls to people who like to receive them. Then both you and the customer will benefit from the call.

- You can reinforce your existing marketing activities with a telephone call to increase awareness of the range of products or services you can provide.

- Customers like to approach you from the comfort of their own home.

- The telephone increases the level of convenience for your customer.

- Even where you are subject to professional or statutory regulations, imaginative use of the telephone helps you to stay in touch with your customers.

IN-HOUSE TRAINING

Branches also do their own training and we feed back to branches how they have been perceived by customers who have phoned. They are measured on their quality of service in terms of how they answer calls. We measure this by, for example, a combination of mystery shopping, questionnaires and alerting them to experiences of regional colleagues who have been passed from department to department. This allows them to seek improvement. We have standards for answering calls quickly, offering names and so on. We encourage them to say it's Barclays and which branch. Then to give the caller their name, particularly if calls are being transferred between sections, so that the customer is alerted to the fact that he is being transferred rather than just hearing clicks on the telephone. The person who picks up the call is encouraged to offer a name and to explain to the customer why he has been put through to him so that at least the customer knows what is happening and there is a sense of continuity. We also try to make transfers acceptable by avoiding the use of bank jargon for department names. We finish the call by thanking the customer and during the call we try to use the customer's name a lot more.

Managing the answering of the telephone is relatively easy when calls are coming in via a switchboard manned with just two or three people, but with hunt groups or situations where the call can be answered by a number of different people the situation is more difficult. It comes down to individuals recognising that the telephone is a vital communication tool. The majority of people can judge you very quickly on how you use the telephone and they do. The old adage of 'pick up the phone and smile' really works, yet so many people don't understand that. They still pick up the phone and say 'just hold on'! I think the problem is that unless your job is based solely around the telephone, it is just another job to you to answer it, it is just another part of your day's work. It's quite easy when you are working at your desk or at a machine and nobody answers the phone. You pick it up and immediately you feel frustrated and you think 'Why didn't someone else pick it up?' so you start off with the wrong attitude. No matter what kind of call it is you start off on the wrong foot.

If you have a dedicated resource where you are going to do nothing but deal with people over the telephone, then training, attitude, everything can be built into it. It's more difficult where you have calls answered by people who have umpteen other things to do and then they are distracted. You do need to give that conversation your undivided attention. A number of people answer the call and carry on working and you can tell.

162

The danger in using outside resources is that the training is perceived as 'external'. It tends not to be taken too seriously. When it comes to service, it needs to be part of the organisation. It needs to be built into the fabric rather than being bolted on. It should be something that is part of the company's life all the time. If your telephone manner is built into your everyday work rather than 'Oh, I've got to remember now to answer the phone in this particular way', then the chance of it going wrong and not hitting the company standards decreases.

We have a number of people who have been trained to deal with complaints that come in by telephone to our regional head office. Inevitably if the complaint is about a branch we don't know the full story so we try to diffuse the situation. By the time it has come to us the caller is quite irate and they feel a bit upset that they have had to come this far. We have to show them that we are going to do something about it and help them to resolve the situation. We monitor the complaints and how they are handled, by using questionnaires.

My personal point of view is that the complaint should be dealt with as near the point of the problem as possible and as quickly as possible. That isn't always practical but I have found from talking to a number of people and from my own experience that the quicker you can grab hold of it and the quicker you can deal with it, the better. It saves your organisation time and effort because dealing with complaints when they come into a system takes a considerable amount of time. Also in terms of the customer's perception of how you have dealt with him, if it has been dealt with quickly and efficiently and as near as possible to the time it happened, the customer will think 'Okay, there was a problem but it has been resolved quickly and efficiently.' If I complain I like things to be solved on the spot. I don't like someone to say it's got to be referred to another department or has to wait because someone isn't available, or wait for two weeks to receive a letter. That's always infuriating.

Learning points

- Introduce telephone standards and measure calls in terms of quality by giving your customers the opportunity to tell you how their calls were handled. Feed this information back to your staff.

- Even where you have high standards on a switchboard, you have to consider how you manage the phone being answered by all employees. Hunt groups push calls through to everybody in a department.

- Telephone training should be perceived as an integral part of the business, not something which is 'bolted on'.

163

- Try to deal with complaints as soon as they are communicated to you. Delays cause more frustration.

John Pettitt – Managing Director, Fraikin Ltd

John Pettitt's company specialises in the contract hire and financing of commercial vehicles. It is the British subsidiary of Europe's largest commercial vehicle contract hire company.

CALLS FROM DISSATISFIED CUSTOMERS

You have to take these calls. You let down your own managers if you don't take these calls because what you're really saying is either I'm not interested or I'm too busy to take this call. Again, you get customers who are already fully aware of what's happened and the outcome, so all you are doing is saying 'I know the situation and I'm supporting my manager'. If you take the role of an MD you have to be supportive to the Sales, Finance and Operations departments so you are talking to all sorts of customers for all sorts of reasons. Very rarely do you talk to someone who rings to say 'I just rang to say what a good job your people are doing'. Life's just not like that!

Your people may have listened to the grievance and decided it's not valid or whatever. If the customer still feels strongly enough to ring up, the only thing you can do is listen. It may well be that in the man pouring out a problem as he sees it there is a germ of a solution that's been missed. I suppose I see my role as being something of an arbiter between my people and customers who are making decisions which are 'black or white'. When those two blacks and whites clash someone has to sit down and work that situation out. So I basically listen. I don't make a decision then and there because if the caller is so determined that he has taken the decision to call you and you make a decision there and then, he will go away feeling aggrieved whatever the decision is.

If you say 'OK you've made a few points, let me take a little time to think about it' he can see you're making the effort. If you are going to turn down his request it allows you to put together the argument you are going to use to reject it. I'm not talking about fobbing people off, I'm talking about presenting an argument that is valid. You may want to say 'I've heard what you've said and you have made a couple of good points'. Try to give them something, it doesn't matter how small, it at least makes the customer understand you've listened to him and it will make them feel better. It is about listening.

When I go back to the customer I would ring them back rather than write. Even if you get involved in a potentially difficult supplier/ customer problem and are 'hurling pieces of paper at each other', there comes a point where you've got to talk. They feel they've got a case – you feel you've got a case. If you don't talk you'll end up in litigation and the only people who win are the lawyers.

Let's face it, we all know that life is a compromise. There's no black and white. People see things and get on their high horse, then they calm down and it's not such a big deal. If you don't talk then eventually it will turn nasty because the fact is that most people – not all people – but most, prefer to talk on a phone or face to face rather than write letters. More people are more comfortable talking than writing a letter. Also a letter, even if 20 pages long, can be covered in five minutes of conversation. In a letter you may well cover unnecessary things.

In a contractual dispute, we start off with the initial letter laying out what has happened and working towards someone saying 'Can we meet?' Depending where you stand, whether you are the aggrieved or not, you may not want to make the first step. It is often seen as weakness, but if no-one makes the first step you end up going nowhere.

I could show you a letter from a private health care organisation where, had the man picked up the phone and explained the problem to me, I could have discussed it with him and we would not now be into our tenth letter. The person I need to speak to does not speak to people, he only writes letters. He is the Customer Services Manager but he doesn't take phone calls. When I asked to speak to him I was told 'He doesn't talk to customers'. He sits in his ivory tower and writes letters. This is not uncommon – I once spoke to the chairman of a national housebuilder to ask him why his sales director would not talk to me on the phone and was told 'He doesn't talk to customers. He's above that sort of thing!' It's a fact of life that these people are often not capable of talking on a face to face basis even though they are considered to be capable of managing certain types of operations.

Like anything else, you get to the point where you see that you're becoming entrenched. It may be that negotiations begin with a letter and you respond with a letter. They may write again and you might decide at that point that a telephone call would be a better means of response. I think that then comes down to how comfortable you are at negotiating, particularly on the telephone. If you are not comfortable on the telephone you will avoid it desperately because you can't predict what the other guy is going to say and he may be more competent than you.

165

Learning points

- If the customer wants to talk to you, take the call.
- Listen carefully to the points the customer wants to make.
- Take time to consider your position. Your customer will appreciate it.
- There comes a point in negotiating a solution where you have to talk.

THE DIFFERENCE BETWEEN TELESALES AND FIELD SALES

I think telesales people have to concentrate 100 per cent. Salesmen can do a 60 per cent performance and get a 90 per cent result because they've got so much going for them. Telesales don't have that advantage, they've only got words to communicate with.

Having been on both sides of the fence, I admire telesales enormously. Being a telesales manager is harder than being a field sales manager. A field sales manager can be supportive and help with the call, but you can't really help a telesales person when they're on the phone. They're trying to think of all the right things to say and the sales people know that the telemanager will be able to say 'Why didn't you say such and such?' With field sales you can help by interjecting with a question. You can't do this with telesales. It is a pure sale and there is no external environment helping you, it's simply two minds communicating and you have to do an awful lot to get that person's attention. The customer probably thinks the call's intrusive so you have to establish the need and you have got to sell to a level where you've then got to post out an order and have them sign it a couple of days later. In telesales there's a natural cooling off period, whereas with field sales when you're face to face you can make out an order and get the customer to sign there and then. For a company, telesales is very cost effective allowing you to present a professional image, even if you don't sell, to a lot of people. A telesales person may make 60 dials a day, 300 a week. With those dials they will probably get through and talk to half that number. They will leave an impression with all 300 and leave a good impression with the 150 they talk to in detail. Field sales make may be 25 calls a week – so if you only look at it as a way of projecting the company, telesales is six times as effective as field sales.

Outside my business I think British business ignores the telephone because they feel uncomfortable. My background is one where the telephone has always been important. In Thomsons I had 150 telesales girls working for me and the telephone was a huge piece of our business. It was so cost effective. Part of the UK problem is that the quality of training is non-existent. 'How to pick up the phone etc'. It's very outdated and doesn't go far enough to be effective. The quality of training in telesales here is not good. Put an advert in the paper to sell something. Watch how many people ring you to try and sell you a better medium to sell that product and listen to the garbage. They are the people who give telesales a bad name.

A reputable wine company, for example, who recently advertised for 'aggressive telephone sales people' missed the point. Aggression has no part in telephone selling. There is a subtle difference between aggressive and assertive. If you are aggressive to a potential customer they will put the phone down. You need to be assertive, not aggressive.

Learning points

- To overcome sales resistance in the UK you need to put good calibre people on the telephone.

- If a salesperson calls you about some facet of your business, listen to what they have to say – they might provide stimulating ideas for you.

- To succeed in telephone selling you need people who can give 100 per cent concentration when on a call.

- Telephone selling allows you to present a professional image to hundreds of people a week for each telesales person you employ.

Mike Hawker – Managing Director, Freemans Mail Order

Freemans is a very large mail order business turning over £600 million. We take orders from over a million agents throughout the year and because of that we need an effective means of getting those orders to us. We particularly need a means of taking orders whereby if somebody orders from us and they are reacting to an offer we've made in the catalogue we need to be able to respond quickly. If they send an order through the post it may take two or three days for that order to get to us. When we get it we will then check the order against our stock records and find that we do not have any stock. We would then have to write back to them, which would take another two to three days, and all we've done after a period of four or five days is to tell a customer we can't meet their requirements.

The obvious solution to that was to introduce the phone into the equation. So ten years ago Freemans introduced the first telephone ordering system for a mail order business in the UK. What that means is a customer can ring up, explain which item she wants, it can be tapped into a screen by the operator, compared to our stock records and then and there we can tell a customer whether the item is in or out of stock. That means we have a much more contented customer. We use an 0345 number so it's a local call rate, although there is an issue that the population generally doesn't understand what an 0345 number actually is. We also use 0800 when we run recruitment ads.

Basically the phone is crucial when you want immediacy – and we believe our customers want to order immediately the goods which they previously obtained by filling out an order form but which didn't actually tell them whether we had the goods. The phone does that. Now, 95 per cent of our orders come by telephone. We are taking about 250,000 calls a week and they are handled in two sites. The level of satisfaction for the customers – and therefore the ability to drive the business into the future – can **only** be met by the phone.

Learning points

- Enabling your customers to use the telephone to place orders speeds up the process and increases customer satisfaction.
- If you use an 0345 number it may be necessary to reinforce the message to your customers that you are paying for some of the cost of the call.
- An 0800 number will encourage potential customers to ring you because the total cost of the call is borne by you.
- A system as sophisticated as the one used by Freemans is expensive but is justified in terms of responding to customer needs rather than to save administration costs.

Because we also give a credit offer to our agents, they will have queries on their accounts, and they can ring us on a different number and have those queries dealt with. I suppose 60 to 70 per cent of those queries now come by phone and a substantial proportion can be dealt with immediately by access to our computer system. They are technically quite small problems but by dealing with them rapidly you prevent them becoming major problems and you don't get correspondence crossing over. Sometimes people don't pay us when they are supposed to and then the phone is a very effective means of chasing the outstanding balances. That direct contact with the customer is far more effective in terms of collecting cash than a letter.

The people who operate our order line clearly have to be trained in basic techniques, keyboard, phone, etc. and need a reasonably pleasant approach. The people who deal with queries have to be even more trained for two reasons. One, because they are going to have more complicated queries and they are possibly going to be confronted by irate customers, and two they have to be able to access our computer system to find out the answers to queries, so if you like, there's a technical ability that is required as well as an inter-relational ability.

Order taking is reasonably straightforward, the only risk is if all the items are out of stock, and you do need good communication ability to deal with that situation. For people who are chasing outstanding balances it's a different issue because it starts off, to a certain extent, as a confrontational situation by its very nature – except it's us at the confrontational end if you like, and so they need to be trained for that.

Learning points

- Customers seek a solution to their queries by telephone rather than by letter.
- Using a different telephone number for enquiries enables Freemans to have operators who specialise in different areas of the business and to develop particular skills to handle those calls.

What we currently do is to say 'No, sorry we haven't got them in stock at the moment – it's due in a couple of weeks'. We don't actually try and do substitute selling. We have a very delicate balance or line to tread as far as our customers are concerned, between maximising the sale and maximising the customer's requirement. To be able to tell the customer 'we haven't got it in red but if you look at page 62 there's one very close' could either be viewed as very useful information by some customers or intrusive by others.

169

We're going to introduce that type of system because I think it better fulfils the customer's requirements and it helps us to utilise our stocks.

Before we do it I would want to look very carefully at the skills of the people we use to take orders and also we would want them to test very carefully the possible reaction of our customers. A lot of people will use mail order because they don't like pushy sales assistants so we've got to make really certain that we don't put a pushy person between them and us.

We are experimenting with some forms of telemarketing which at the moment are mainly in the form of add on sales, not substitute sales. At the moment we just need to modify our systems slightly and also build some substantial data because it's no good trying to do substitute selling unless you've got very good data behind you. If you do refer somebody to page 62 you have to be certain that what you are referring them to is correct! I would see it far more as us giving information to encourage someone to take a further action. If by saying to somebody 'look at page 62' they say 'if you think it's right, just order it for me' then fine. As an example of add on sales, we sell electrical goods, eg tape recorders. They don't necessarily have batteries so an obvious add on is to say 'do you want some batteries?'

Learning points

- Substitute selling is a desirable company objective but first it is important to test your customers' reaction.

- You need to identify the training needs of your staff and develop a programme to meet them when they are asked to develop the call further.

- Your systems need to be adequate to support any changes you want to introduce into the transaction.

- Experimenting and testing customer reaction will help you to make the right decisions.

We also sell extended warranties. We do a mailing and then follow up with a telephone call. We have got to look carefully at the trade off between the amount of time we spend taking an order and the value inherent in that order so the main thrust of our order taking operations is to get the number of lines per operator as high as possible because that is a measure of our efficiency. The longer we extend the phone call the less productive we become so we think it's better to target the extended warranty by post and then follow up, through the telephone, the people who have received mailings.

Typically that increases the number of people who take up the offer.

Learning point

- A high volume of incoming calls demands a careful consideration of the balance between being available to answer those calls quickly and maximising the time you spend talking to your customers.

Our telephone lines are open seven days a week, 24 hours a day. It needs very effective management, both people management and technological management. We have got sophisticated call handling on two sites that distributes calls on a first come first served basis. It provides a queueing arrangement but it also gives us enormous amounts of data on which to make future staffing decisions. What we are looking to do is to get in balance the number of staff we have at any time with the number of calls that need to be taken in order to get the maximum utilisation of staff and the minimum negative reaction by abandoned calls.

When we first started we used external resources but now we do the training ourselves so if a new operator comes in we use an existing operator to train them. If we've got new systems or new operational methods then we use our training department in conjunction with the manager of telephone handling operations.

The need to use an external agency would arise if we wanted to do something different, if we wanted to start doing something that previously we hadn't done and we believed that the interactive processes were more complex than those we had previously used. Then I think we would be very wise to look outside the business. At the moment most of what we do is limited to a a reactive process and the more pro-active we become the more that means major changes as far as we are concerned and we would then need to seek some external advice. What I would then expect is that once we had got people properly trained we would revert to our in-house training. We don't want to bring in external trainers every time we recruit four or five new staff.

In the next couple of years we will move to a more pro-active stance with our customers because I think people will see it as supportive rather than intrusive and what we will do is identify on our systems those customers who react favourably so we don't telephone people who don't want it. Obviously there is going to be new technology developing over the next four or five years. I would still see the phone as continuing to be the most important medium that we would have available to us to communicate with our customers. I don't see a computer screen in the home really coming to the fore in that period. The continuation of the telephone and a catalogue or some other medium still makes enormous sense. We will use the telephone in more and more imaginative ways as we move forward.

171

Learning points

- Call distribution systems help you to understand the peaks and flows of incoming call traffic into your business.
- Use external resources to train staff in new activities but develop in-house resources to meet future ongoing demand.
- Target activity to customers who respond positively to such calls.

Liz Morse – Telemarketing Manager

Liz Morse is a Telemarketing Manager for a market leader in the contract hire of company vehicles market. What follows is an account of how the company developed customer use of their daily rental facility.

THE DAILY RENTAL DEPARTMENT

The selling process begins with a mailing being sent out to each of our prospective customers and is addressed to the fleet controller. Actually discovering who is responsible for purchasing is part of the task of each daily rental consultant. It is very important that they are trained in good questioning techniques so that they can identify correctly who the decision maker is. The mailing is sent with a covering letter explaining all about the service. It indicates that a consultant will contact the client in the next couple of days. The mailing is staggered appropriately to ensure that the telephone call takes place no later than three days after the mailing has arrived. Experience has shown that telephone calls following a mailing need to be made three days maximum after they have arrived otherwise the two things don't become connected in a customer's head. They are more likely to have thrown the letter away and it isn't fresh in their mind.

The telephone call serves to reiterate the message sent in our marketing literature and then through skilled questioning we find out the needs of our customer with regard to daily rental requirements. This is then followed up, if a need is identified, with a tariff card and further sales calls.

Obviously we employ sales techniques to persuade customers that they should be using us for their daily rental needs. We use features and benefits and unique sales points.

This has proved remarkably successful, by raising awareness of the customers to this service we have found that six per cent of the people who thought they had no need subsequently ordered from us. With a product like daily rental it is very immediate, it's an instant response. Awareness is raised very quickly but that awareness has to be maintained because we can also be forgotten very quickly so we now have a programme of call backs where even customers who say they have no need are called back every six months. The effectiveness of this campaign indicates so far that, in a shrinking market (our current suppliers estimate that the market has shrunk by five per cent in the last six months) our repeat business, without the activity and use promoted by the daily rental department, would account for only 30 per cent of our profits. Against that background, the planned activity that was agreed for the department was estimated to produce a profit of £144,914 for 1992/1993, and we've actually made £74,000 this year. It has been an extremely effective way of doing business. Twenty four per cent of the people we contact buy daily rental from us, which is a phenomenal 'strike' rate.

The team at the moment is only very small. There is myself as daily rental manager and two daily rental consultants. One concentrates on the larger accounts. She services the accounts and is also tasked with investigating the rental activity from customers who hire without having spoken to us first. It is important that we get a handle on that business and understand it. The other consultant is an experienced salesperson but is, if you like, cutting his teeth on the day to day contacting of our core clients and he has been very successful so far. He has contributed at least £3,000 a month to our total profit revenue.

173

The department is new and we are still learning about how the business works. One of the prime motivators for the team has been the creation of the department. The very fact that they are involved in the start of the department opens up opportunities for them. Personal development and career progression, which they wouldn't necessarily be able to achieve in an established sales environment, makes it new and exciting for them and they feel very much a part of the team.

Learning points

- Opportunities to do business with existing customers can be enhanced by using the telephone to identify new markets or to develop existing ones.

- Low usage of an existing facility can be stimulated by pro-active telephone contact.

- If you say you are calling your customer in three days, stagger your mailing activity to enable you to do so. Otherwise you are in danger of creating a negative impression on your customers.

- A telephone call reinforces your mailing activity.

- In a shrinking market you can develop your business by increasing market share and the amount of 'repeat' business you get through promoting your service via the telephone.

- Use the calls to establish why people buy. It helps you to achieve a better understanding of your business.

- A new venture for your company benefits from the commitment and enthusiasm of the people who are charged with making it work. Telephone skills previously unused can be channeled more profitably even within a very small team.

Elizabeth Daykin – Senior Collections Manager, Club 24

Club 24 specialises in the management of millions of small transactions round the clock for 365 days a year. It is a bureau which manages credit or any other type of high volume, telephone based operations for other companies. This is what Elizabeth Daykin, their Senior Collections Manager, has to say.

174

Traditionally the people who were recruited for collection were aggressive people. They were told 'you will do this'. That situation has changed. Customers are more credit aware and you get, in my experience, three types of customers. Ones who won't pay, the ones who are embarrassed you are ringing them, and the ones with genuine difficulties. You need lots of skills to cover these situations, especially when people are embarrassed by the situation they can be aggressive, so staff will actively listen and explore the customer's situation. You need to check the understanding of the client during the conversation and summarise the action points involved and the consequences if those things don't happen.

In the past, the telephone training for collection staff was of the 'you will pay' variety and treated customers as the lowest of the low. We have changed this profile and how we speak to our customers. The end result is that we have increased our collections. You don't have to be rude and aggressive which is how it used to be.

Over a six month period we have increased the amount of money collected by five per cent and productivity by seven per cent because our staff now feel in control. A lot of it is about confidence. If you are not confident on the phone or not sure of your facts, it does come across to a customer. There is nothing wrong with saying 'I will ring you back' if you are struggling. The calls take longer now because they are actually getting to the bottom line of what the customer is going to do to resolve the situation.

Following coaching we introduced quality control. We tried to introduce quality control before coaching and it didn't work. Whilst the standards were there, people didn't have the skills for quality control. The supervisors check 30 calls per month for each member of staff and they have a checklist to ensure that all the relevant points are covered, eg did they explore the situation? Are the necessary measures carried out, etc. This maintains standards across the department. The staff have been made more accountable because previously any decision that was outside the norm, less than a monthly payment, for example, had to be made by a supervisor. They can now negotiate within certain parameters and this gives them much more flexibility. We check that they don't go straight for the bottom line by regular coaching.

175

We also provide incentives for our staff. A percentage of revenue achieved over the target forms a pool. We measure productivity, quality and results. For example there are lots of calls which last a short time. This would indicate that no negotiation is taking place. If calls are too long it would indicate that the caller is probably not controlling the call. I will look at and analyse the calls which err either side because this helps me to identify training needs. Some people can't do a collections job but I think it's a selling job, not a telling job. We look for somebody who is calm, assertive, an individual who can cope with stress and pressure and can demonstrate how they cope. We don't want aggressive people, we want assertive people who can negotiate and we examine their attitudes to being supervised and working as part of a team. It is attitude and how they work as part of a team that really counts. I won't refuse to recruit someone because they have no previous office experience. It's their life skills that are important to me.

I was spending too much time on the telephone so I had to train my supervisors to deal with situations by being more assertive and using listening skills with everyone so that they could handle those situations. I see my staff now as being more accountable. The supervisors were given permission to be responsible for their own actions and they should be able to deal with awkward customers, not in an aggressive way because you get into a lose-lose situation. They have been retrained to deal with those sort of calls and when they think they can't, you go through a coaching process with them to identify where they are going wrong. They forget about breathing techniques. We spend a lot of time going through how they can project their voice and how to listen.

We introduced what we called a 'coaching workshop' where we looked at how we gave feedback to staff, how to deal with aggressive customers, body language – even on the telephone there is a lot of body language which is unconscious. We have a coaching sheet which covers all these areas and everyone in the department has been coached in these techniques.

Learning points

- To be effective when approaching collection calls, you need to recruit people who can demonstrate an understanding of the client and who are able to summarise action points and the consequences of failure to carry them out.

- Coach first, then introduce quality control.
- Measuring productivity, quality and results helps you to analyse and identify training needs.
- It's a selling job, not a telling job.
- Training your supervisors to handle situations cuts down the amount of time you spend dealing with calls yourself.

Barbara Wakefield – Marketing Services Manager for Club 24

We run in-house training courses on customer care and skills-based training on how to answer a telephone. We have brought in external consultants to develop the skills necessary to achieve better communication by telephone. The training is extensive and can last six to seven weeks. It has been a change of culture, the style is much more relaxed.

The first week is an induction into the business. Anyone joining our organisation needs to understand who we are and what we do, the structure, what our resource is and the technology and telephones. Further training on customer care and telephone technique is module based and may reaffirm what they already know or teach them something new. We cannot evaluate that until we begin training.

We have a prompting system for an operator and we rely on the training techniques to have delivered information that they need to have the dialogue with the client. A customer wouldn't get a script read to them – it would be a very free and easy flow of dialogue. We don't give them the words to use. They use their own style, their own accent. The customer is talking to someone who can help. We are not rigid at all, we don't try and formalise the approach so we are not looking for a formal delivery which they might get in some organisations. We are looking for a friendly approach. If it takes ten minutes, fine. If it takes 20 minutes, fine. We want people to go off the phone thinking that they have been given all the information they need to go out and buy the service. As soon as the operator puts the phone down, all the necessary paperwork will go to the customer for completion and sending back, and that's it. That's how it works.

Learning points

- Today's style of dealing with customers on the telephone is less rigid and more relaxed.
- Training is extensive. A comprehensive induction course is followed by module-based training which focuses on specific areas.
- A free and easy flow of dialogue with customers is encouraged.
- Prompts, rather than scripts, are used.
- The company has developed a support system which enables the transactions to be completed by post and which is actioned as soon as the call is completed.

Anthony Costello – Deputy Group Administrator

Anthony Costello is a Deputy Group Administrator in the pension department of a large authority in the North West

People ring the department for guidance about pensions and super-annuation. Most of the calls are internal or from managers in other authorities.

We have guidance notes that advise you take a caller's name and give your name and number if the caller needs to get back. It also encourages ownership of the problem which is a development of customer care practice. It makes sure that you don't refer people around other departments. That used to happen a lot but as customer care has had its profile raised in the last ten years that sort of thing has lessened. People don't want to be diverted, they want to speak to somebody who is going to help carry it through for them and who is going to get back to them. If we can't answer a query we will get back to them rather than them get back to us. We deal with a lot of pensioners so what we try to do is take the onus off them. Pensioners don't like using the telephone and so we try to make it as easy as possible for them.

I'm glad to say I can't remember the last time I had a complaint from a customer. I think that is because there is much greater awareness of telephone communication and how it affects customer care. Recently I reacted with speed to the need for a member of my staff to have extra telephone coaching. Ten years ago I don't think we would have worried too much about it. There is the recognition now that a telephone call is a direct communication with your customer and you have to make a good impression – you had **better** make a good impression – because it may be the first and only chance you've got. The standard needs to be good and where it is not, something is done about it. It works well now, there is a great awareness.

We have devised a form to complete, which records a conversation and what we need to know, to assist staff when they do receive calls. Often people don't know what they should do with the information and what they should be asking for to deal with a query from a pensioner. They would need to make a note of the caller's name, our reference number, where the caller works and the nature of the query, who they think the enquiry is for, who they are going to pass the enquiry to and whether they need to respond. The form works really well and it is a good reminder to staff to collect the right information.

We don't have a switchboard and all the calls come in on direct lines. The telephone number listed in the directory is the one that comes into my team. Sometimes this causes difficulties in that we get enquiries about things we don't deal with, as we work in a satellite office and the rest of the department is elsewhere. We have talked a number of times about getting a helpline but the variety of work is such that it is better to stay with one number and so we continue to take calls backed up by good procedures to get back to customers or to transfer calls. To make a helpline work we would need staff with enough experience to answer any kind of query and we can make better use of those staff elsewhere. A helpline would be of limited use as callers who come in via a telephone directory are small in number because pensioners can contact us via the telephone number on their payslip and employers via a liaison officer who would have the appropriate telephone numbers for everyone in the department.

Members and pensioners also phone direct. I've noticed that people are increasingly using the telephone to solve their problems rather than writing. We now have a direct dialling system and if people know they can get directly through to you without being diverted or put on hold, they will get in touch with you.

Learning points

- Give your staff written guidelines that clearly state the standards you require so that everyone knows what is expected of them.

- If you identify staff who need extra telephone coaching, organise it immediately. You will limit the damage caused by poor customer relations.

- To improve the handling of queries, use a form which sets out the information that needs to be gathered. It helps to avoid the need to call your customer back to fill in the gaps.

- Helplines are useful but if you have a limited resource and the queries require your most experienced staff to deal with them, it is more practical to have one central point of contact and to redirect calls from there.

- Do everything you can to help your customers contact the appropriate member of staff directly. Print telephone numbers on any material your customers are likely to see.

179

Andy Ray – Customer Services Manager, Vernons Pools

BACKGROUND TO ORGANISATION

We were founded in 1926 and we celebrated our 66th anniversary last year. For the first sixty-one years of our operation we were privately owned by the Sangster family and are now part of the Ladbroke organisation. We have about 1000 people working in Vernons including a lot of casual people who come in on a Saturday to process the coupons.

Approximately two million people use Vernons pools every week. Most are regular clients and some play one week and not the next.

It is fair to say that this is an industry where the standard of service to customers has been low and the telephone operation was one of the ways we could differentiate from our competitors by offering our customers a good service.

The whole operation was started completely from scratch. We sensed there was a need for customers to be able to play by telephone but before we invested in the staff, training and equipment etc. we wanted to prove that there was a market for it. So in the first instance, we had an agency working on our behalf who handled the calls for us and it proved quite successful. We were getting 2500 to 3000 calls a week. We recognised there was a need for it and so in 1991 we took it over from them.

The major difference between using an internal resource rather than an agency was the fact that we had taken ownership of it. We took great pride in not missing any calls and provided good service, whereas the agency acted as a message taking service. We can give the clients the answers they want when they are on the telephone but the agency had to give them another number to phone, which wasn't ideal.

The starting point was to take renewals on the telephone. Then we began to handle coupon requests. People had to phone an 0800 number to ask for coupons. This year we have also started to take new bets by telephone. As well as other information we are actually taking a client's score draw numbers from them, which is quite a revolutionary thing because for the first sixty-four years of its history the pools have been a wholly paper-based operation!

Three weeks before a client's standing entry is due to be renewed, we write to them offering them the chance to renew it. Incorporated on that coupon and subsequently flashed over the envelope is the fact that we have a freephone number to allow them to renew by telephone. Only credit and debit card holders can use it. If a client renews he can bet for ten weeks at say £2 a week and his credit card will be debited by £20. The average length is around fifteen weeks.

We've been taking it stage by stage and making sure we have been happy handling the inbound side of things very efficiently, so now we're ready to go on to the next stage of things, which is for us to use the telephone in a more pro-active manner. We have already had several experiments and some we have already done are in relation to generating syndicate leads for our field force, where we have rung such outlets as Threshers, Bulmers Cider and Little Chef. We have phoned all their outlets and asked them if they have received the materials for our promotion and asked how it is going and whether they would like to run a collectorship or a syndicate in their place of work.

If they are interested, we take details and pass them on to our collector service department and they send out a manager to follow up the lead. We called five hundred Little Chef outlets and we got a 58 per cent conversion to the leads. From Threshers we got 34 per cent from between five and six hundred calls, so we are achieving some spectacular results.

Our collector service also sends out mailshots to businesses. We use telesales after two or three weeks have gone by to telephone people who haven't responded. The hard part of this exercise is trying to find the person you need to speak to. It's not necessarily the manager – it could be someone in the canteen or someone on the production line, but it's very rewarding when we do get through to them. We have a strike rate of anywhere between 20 and 30 per cent. When we phone somebody and say we're from Vernons Pools, there is an immediate glow that comes over the line. They know the name and the call starts off with a bit of a laugh – 'Oh, have I won?' and it gets the conversation off to a good start. Previously we didn't telephone non-responders to our direct mail campaigns but with a 20 to 30 per cent uptake we will definitely continue to do so in the future.

We have about 70,000 customers who are due to renew their bets each week and we can identify those people who lapse. There is an element of attrition and we phone people to encourage them back into the pools. We are in the process of data capturing telephone numbers at present but it is quite labour intensive. The database was originally geared to direct mail. Now with its increased telephone activity, we need to bolt the telephone number on. We want to go further with this because we encourage about 15 per cent to come back into the pool.

We currently get between 12,000–14,000 calls a week. That's grown from the 2500 we started out with twelve months ago. We have completed the process of switching over our renewals telephone line to an 0800 number from an 051 number so clients are able to phone us and renew at no cost to themselves. We expect that to significantly uplift our business by as much as between 10 and 20 per cent. Our new bet line has always been 0800.

Our strategy is to make ourselves more accessible to our customers. Before, customers could only find the Vernons number via Directory Enquiries so you can imagine that by the time they got through to us they were already pretty fed up. We went into a halfway situation in August 1992. We offered an 0345 number but I believe our customers didn't realise we were paying 80 per cent of the call. We decided to go the whole hog and reap the full benefit of offering the service. From January 1993 anybody who wants to get through to Vernons can do so on a free basis and they can find our number splattered over the coupon. Our service is available from 8.00 am to 8.00 pm, seven days a week.

We now have over 70 telephone sales people working on a part-time basis. We have benefitted from being able to recruit experienced telesales people and we have a first rate team which is a credit to our company. One of the things they like, is that coming to work is a pleasure because when they are on the telephone talking to our clients, as they go through the transaction, they get a lot of compliments. People say how great the service is, how much better it is than when they had to post the coupon and 'Is it that simple?' or 'Is that it?' or 'Don't you want anything else from me?' is often heard. They have a wonderful time fielding the compliments. Calls average out at between three and four minutes with about fifteen seconds between each call, so a telesales operator can take about one hundred calls in a five-hour shift.

New employees undergo a rigorous training programme and we have regular ongoing training. The current induction course lasts one week but it will increase to two weeks to take account of the new activities we are taking on board. They also have a programme of visits to enable them to understand what goes on elsewhere in the business, particularly those who are on the customer service lines. They learn about what concerns our customers through talking to people who deal with customer written enquiries and who have a great deal of experience. Training is a vital part of our service. Product knowledge is very important. We can't give them all the information they need in a week so it is a matter of training on an ongoing basis.

Our telephone operation isn't going to replace our collector service. However, the massive headway it has made, even in a year, from 2 to 3 per cent of customers who were due to renew, doing so by telephone, to a figure of over 10 per cent today, ensures that it will remain an integral part of our business. It offers an alternative service for clients making it as easy as possible for them to do business with us and it provides a friendly touch. Approximately 12,000 people contact us every week, they get a warm friendly response and hopefully encourage their friends to use this service. Our telesales team improves the service we give and helps us to keep our customers.

Learning points

- In the first two years calls to the company have increased from 2000–3000 to between 12,000 and 14,000 calls.
- The introduction of an 0800 number on Vernons renewal line has increased business by 10 to 20 per cent.
- From being a paper-based operation they have identified opportunities in all areas of the business:
  - Renewals
  - New Bets
  - Generating Syndicate Leads for the Sales Force
  - Calling non-responders to mail shots
  - Handling general enquiries
  - Reducing attrition amongst existing customers.
- The telephone helps Vernons to provide a service which demonstrates to their customers that they are 'a nice company to deal with'.

183

All the people who have contributed to the closing section of this book are committed to good telephone communication in their business. Their experience of managing telephone contact in different organisations demonstrates how, by approaching the use of the telephone in an imaginative way, they have been able to gain a greater understanding of the needs of their customers and their employees.

I know you will now be tempted to put some of the ideas you have been given into practice. Try them – *they work*!

Index

■

185